"Dr. Hemphill has been int[...] his insight and expertise to [...] conditioned reactions, and emotional patterns that no longer serve you."

—Dr. Reina Santiago, *DOM*

"*Four Faces in the Mirror*, a much needed simple book, is geared toward the lay person. Seekers of personal transformation will gain much insight into their selves and create a foundation for attaining Grace...."

—Irene Watson, *Reader Views*

"Vito's book *Four Faces in the Mirror* offers us many golden nuggets for seeing ourselves more clearly. His words offer guidance for growing more conscious and empowered as men and woman."

—Peri Coeurtney Enkin, Author of *Love Letters from Your Higher Self*

"Vito Hemphill's book gives excellent descriptions of the essence of masculinity and femininity, including their shadow aspects. It also provides a helpful technique about how to balance these opposites inside and outside ourselves."

—Sabine Lucas, Ph.D., author of *Past Life Dreamwork: Healing the Soul through Understanding Karmic Patterns*

"*Four Faces in the Mirror* is a useful, refreshing, straightforward set of focused ideas and sharp exercises... I really liked the way he avoided the triple plagues of theology, ideology, and California syrup. A real American book, pragmatic."

John Allen, Founder of *Biosphere 2* and author of *Me and the Biospheres*

"... extraordinary and informative ... I definitely hope to hear more from this author. Two thumbs up!"

—Brian Whitmoyer, *Polaris Reviews*

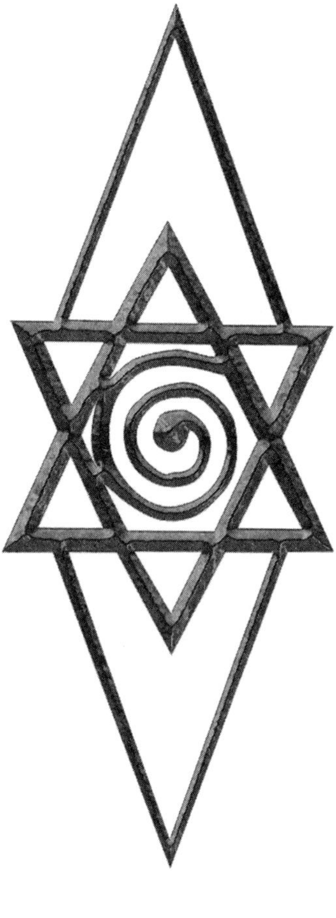

This book is dedicated to all those
who are willing to take an honest
look at themselves and to make the
changes needed to enjoy life more fully.

For private phone consultations, workshops,
lectures, DVD, and other materials related to
the concepts presented in this book,
please contact Dr. Hemphill at:
www.vitohemphill.com

FOUR FACES IN THE MIRROR:

SEEING ALL OF YOURSELF

VITO HEMPHILL DC

Llumina Press

© 2008 Vito Hemphill

All rights reserved. No part of this publication may be reproduced or transmitted in any form or by any means electronic or mechanical, including photocopy, recording, or any information storage and retrieval system, without permission in writing from both the copyright owner and the publisher.

Requests for permission to make copies of any part of this work should be mailed to Permissions Department, Llumina Press, PO Box 772246, Coral Springs, FL 33077-2246

ISBN: 978-1-60594-079-3 (PB)
       978-1-60594-080-9 (HC)
       978-1-60594-081-6 (Ebook)

Printed in the United States of America by Llumina Press

Library of Congress Control Number: 2008904628

Table of Contents

Acknowledgments	i
Foreword	iii
Introduction	xi
The Original Separation of Masculine and Feminine	1
Seeing Within Self	5
Feminine Energy	11
The Dark Feminine	19
Masculine Energy	23
The Dark Masculine	31
Feminine Nectar	35
Masculine Boundaries	39
Seeing Within Your Lover	45
Seeing Within External Relationships	51
The Inner Balance	55
Inner Dialog	63
Being While Doing	67
Grace	75
Practical Exercises	79
Externalizing Inner Balance	97
Worksheets	103

Acknowledgments

I would first like to thank my chiropractic patients for teaching me the basic principles of healing. Their pain and their personal stories have been the impetus for me to develop my abilities as a healer. The processes presented in this book are a result of time spent with patients combined with my personal life experience.

I would especially like to thank my editor, Cindee Pascoe, for the special attention she gave to my project. Her writing talent profoundly enriched the depth and clarity of this book so that I could more effectively express myself.

My friend, Doug Coffin, contributed his amazing art as the cover image. He is a renowned American contemporary Indian artist who lives in New Mexico. His paintings, sculpture, and jewelry have inspired me for several decades. I am honored to share his work with you.

Finally, I would like to thank Brenda DuCharme for doing the final proof reading and for helping me to get this book published. Brenda has taught me that simple peaceful passion is a solid foundation for the experience of more grace in my life.

Foreword

I was born in Pittsburgh, Pennsylvania, in 1957, to parents who were very conservative and emotionally quite opposite. Mom was a nurse until she met my dad, the doctor, and she quickly retired by age twenty-seven to be the housewife and mother (the idealized dream of that era). I was the oldest of two children and there were many problems around our house. Dad delivered babies and was gone often for days in a row. Mom got depressed and ate more each year. She stayed in her room to lie in bed watching TV and reading romance novels. Sometimes she would stay in there for days.

By the time I was six, I was already having problems at school with other children beating me. I never fought back. Somehow I knew that hitting wasn't right and I should not do that to others. I tried not to share any of my pain with my mom because she was already hurting with her own problems. I never cried until I was twenty-five. I believed early on that the best way to help others was to keep my own pain to myself and do what everyone else needed.

My father was absent. He never went to my school to defend me. He was a good doctor and the breadwinner. My friends always said, "You have it so good, your dad's a doctor and you live in a big house." Inside, I did not feel so lucky or happy. I felt nervous, repressed, and empty. I focused on my academic work and many hobbies. I used singing to stay alive. I sang in church choirs from age six until I was twenty. I know now that this literally kept my throat alive when I couldn't cry or scream or get any emotions out of my body. I was an emotional mess and I didn't even know it.

I did pre-med and joined the sex, drugs, and rock and roll scene at age eighteen when I left home to go to college. I started to see myself through this new lens of other people and altered states. I began to feel pain for the first time in my life. I felt really unsafe and nervous at being away from my family (even though they didn't know how to help me). I felt cut off from life. I couldn't keep up with all the studies, parties, and emotions. I finally burned out and left school two years later feeling like a failure. I went back home to attend the University of Pittsburgh where my studies improved and the frequency of parties decreased. I met the eventual mother of my three children. It was a karmic relationship filled with volatile emotions. There were many challenges throughout the eighteen years of our marriage. I didn't seek help through counseling until I was twenty-seven.

In 1975, I developed an interest in what used to be called 'holistic health.' I focused mostly on nutrition and yoga. I started practicing simple hatha yoga which allowed me to become deeply aware of my physical body for the first time in my life. I adopted a vegetarian diet, took nutritional supplements, and drank purified water. I started to change my consciousness and improve the health of my body by these simple actions.

Five years later, I went to chiropractic college to learn the science that was at the root of my healthy lifestyle changes. My first college was known for being the most scientifically focused, but it lacked in technique training. I transferred to a school in Oregon to pursue a more holistic chiropractic education that taught healing modalities. The students who were attracted to living in Oregon were very nature-oriented. Being in Oregon was the first time I lived in nature and went to the hot springs in the national forest. This wilderness experience was an essential part of my personal growth process.

I enjoyed the emotional depth that I experienced with patients in the school clinic and I got several jobs doing massage therapy while attending school. My special interest was acupressure and the study of the acupuncture meridian system. I found that by applying pressure to one point, an entire muscle spasm could be released. I was also a campus representative for a professional nutritional company. This encouraged me to study nutrition on my own.

Since my dad was a successful medical doctor at the University of Pittsburgh Medical Center, I had been raised in a sophisticated western medical community and my family's friends were other doctors. I had never experienced chiropractic adjustments or alternative healing methods. My studies at chiropractic college were shattering the limiting beliefs I learned from my childhood. I attended off-campus seminars and read unusual books. I have always remained respectful of medical science and the value of allopathic medicine because it is necessary with certain problems such as trauma, infection, complicated childbirth, serious long term diseases, and for many other situations. There is a place for all forms of healing. Each patient needs different modalities.

As I continued exploring, my interest began to shift to the emotional and spiritual aspects of healing. For over twenty years and into the present time, my personal counseling experiences have included re-birthing, talk therapy, Jungian therapy, channeled therapy, shamanic therapy, marriage counseling, intuitive readings, astrological readings, numerological readings, tarot readings, child-family counseling, past life memory therapy, and many medicinal plant ceremonies with shamans and alone.

I began to realize that most dis-ease begins with disturbances on the emotional and spiritual levels before illness appears in the physical body. Many of the popular writers of the early 1980's started naming 'stress' as the real cause of disease. 'Stress' was the culprit. But, who was he, she, or it? What were you to do about such an affliction? I assumed that specific sources of diseases were issues such as fear, anger, greed, pride, gluttony, lust, or low self-esteem. I felt that sick people needed to somehow identify their specific emotional challenges and then they could consciously work with those issues to promote better physical health.

My question was how to accurately identify which deeper emotional and spiritual issues were causing what problems. By the mid-80's, books started to be written which listed emotional causes of specific diseases. Each disease supposedly had a specific emotional source. One example was arthritis. The premise was that if you had arthritis, you probably had a rigid or controlling personality. Rigidity in the emotions supposedly caused rigidity in the physical body. It all seemed simple enough. If you had a chart, you could look up your condition and it would tell you what emotional problem was causing the symptoms.

I started looking at these suggested relationships with most of my patients beginning in 1985. I found that there was a significant correlation with the chart in many cases, but it was not always correct. This made me realize that there had to be a way to gain more specific information. I decided that my clinical goal was to literally bring what was 'un-conscious' and 'sub-conscious' into full consciousness using each patient's inner guidance.

I learned how to do muscle testing in the mid-80's and later I developed an 'asking process' using symbols of the Kabala to determine chiropractic adjustments. In 1995, I wrote a clinical manual entitled, **Subtle Body Balancing** which is available as an e-book on my website. This text outlines the procedures used in the 'asking process' and is intended to teach practitioners how to do this work. I continue to teach this process to other therapists in my practitioner's training program. **Subtle Body Balancing** includes the multiple meaning of the symbols, clinical questions, testing procedures, therapeutic exercises, and patient examples. The practical course provides hands on experience with patients and testing procedures.

More recently I realized that there is another way to reach the sub-conscious to release unhealthy patterns and physical disease which is the subject of this book. Every person, man or woman, has both masculine and feminine aspects. A healthy balance of both results in healthy inner balance which leads to emotional maturity and physical health. Stress and disease of all kinds can be traced back to wounding of these aspects during the early years of life.

I would like to summarize the development of my emotional-spiritual self in regard to the subject of this book. My personal process has been my teacher. It has been my inspiration to show others how to access and heal their own emotional wounds to lead a more fulfilling and less stressful life. When I first started to become aware of myself, both my masculine and feminine aspects were badly wounded and un-empowered. My earliest message from my parents was to keep the pain inside and not to scream or cry. "Never tell the neighbors" was the rule in our home. The role I took on at too early an age was to be the caretaker and emotional support person. I learned to be hyper-vigilant for my mother and my younger sister. I learned that no matter what I did to help, it wasn't enough to fix or save others. I became systematically co-dependent. I wasn't happy if they were suffering. I couldn't suffer out loud because they couldn't handle it.

My mom decided by the time I was eight weeks old that I was the kind of child that didn't want to be held. She stopped breastfeeding me on the second day of my life. She never did either the holding or breastfeeding again. My father was constantly physically absent because he was working. I had a strong early message that no one was there for me and I could not trust anyone to support me even for the basics in life. I didn't understand this emotionally or mentally. I was completely shut down in constant nervousness. I thought all this was normal and my friends re-assured me that I was one of the fortunate ones.

I did not begin to consciously look at my own emotional issues until I started to seek counseling at age twenty-seven, nearly at the end of my chiropractic training. The first thing I explored was the pain I had suffered at the abandonment of my family. The result was that my emotions became much more available to me and I could begin to feel for the first time ever. I literally opened the flood gates of tears. But, I also would get very irritated and then shut down again. These cycles of release, anger, and shut-down seemed to come and go every few months. I was getting in touch with what I now know is 'the victimization of the feminine.'

I used therapy as a way to reflect my patterns back to myself. I started to see cause and effect. I saw how what was not dealt with sub-consciously became manifest physically. I learned how I 'attracted' other people that were the same or opposite of where I was finding myself emotionally and spiritually. I also continued to study Kabala and to meditate to see the bigger picture, and to learn by observing what was happening around me.

When I was thirty-three, people started to tell me I was angry. My response was something like, "I'm a nice guy and I don't get angry." As I looked deeper into myself, I realized that it was true and that I was really enraged. I was furious. I even imagined smashing my children against the wall until their blood rolled down the plaster. These horrific thoughts showed me I really needed help. My intuition said, "Get a short barrel shotgun and do target practice to move the rage." I had a lot of resistance to this idea because I didn't like guns and I especially did not like men with guns. My intuition suggested that my resistance was a sign of how powerful such a process could be for me. I bought such a gun, an ax, and protective clothing. For eight weeks, I sat down and started to think about some of the things that made me mad. In no time at all, I was feeling the rage. Then, I picked up the ax and started to chop deadwood out of the trees. I used my big boots to kick the deadwood out of trees and I shot my shotgun at pine cone targets in the woods.

At first, I was scared by the gun and gradually I began to like it and the power that it had. I realized that I was a barbarian like so many other hurting men. I also realized that I had a choice to be powerful and not to hurt others, as I moved the vital energy that was trapped behind my rage. This opened up my positive masculine energy in a whole new way. One day as I was shooting, I fell to the ground and started to cry. It seemed that finally the rage had passed and I was opening to my own heart in a new and fuller way. I felt more empowered and less like a victim. Once the masculine aspect in me started to function as the 'protector masculine' I was able to go deeper into my grief. My masculine self now protected my still-wounded feminine self and 'she' was able to cry from a deeper and fuller place.

All of this feminine-masculine balance correction started to bring forth a greater feeling of true joy in my heart. It has been seventeen years since my rage first began to be addressed. It has taken time for most of these subtle blocks to be released. By releasing emotional and mental patterns from my past, everything in my life now feels lighter and more delightful. I feel more like I can consciously act instead of react to situations in my life. This is very empowering. I feel that my masculine and feminine aspects are both healthier now after these years of processing and therapy.

The current focus of my personal evolution is the fine balancing of my masculine and feminine aspects. My work is now about embodying the essence of the following aspects of divine love: appreciation, compassion, forgiveness, humility, understanding, and valor to balance anything challenging that arises in life. This process has led me to recently end my second marriage. As a result of seeing myself more clearly, I was able to calmly, clearly, and consciously end what was a stuck pattern. Rather than seeing the divorce as a failure, I am choosing to see it as an opportunity for both myself and my former wife to do the healing and growing we both need to do to be more aware and loving partners in future relationships. I find that the level of drama in my life is reducing all the time. Simplicity and a greater sense of peacefulness have largely replaced so many old stories that used to be true. It will be interesting to consciously experience where it all goes from here.

The mirror is always there and I just need to stay fully conscious of 'who is standing right in front of me' on a moment to moment basis. I have to see through my own eyes, which have been affected by my own past and my own pain. My intention is to continue to grow and to bring whatever is sub-conscious and un-conscious into full consciousness to support positive changes.

The goal of this book is to show people how they can do much of this deeper inner work themselves using techniques which help identify emotional wounding in their own masculine and feminine aspects. This work is exciting and rewarding, both for individuals and for the potential healing of relationships of all kinds. Both men and women can learn how to look at their own internal balance using the methods presented in this book. I am also offering private phone consultations, workshops, and lectures on this material for more personal exploration. You can contact me directly for private phone consultations and check out a schedule of my upcoming seminars at: www.vitohemphill.com.

I hope that these techniques and insights will bring abundant healing and rich joy into your life. This work is all about becoming more aware of yourself and using that awareness to positively change yourself and your larger experience of life.

Introduction

People are beginning to realize that we create our physical realities based on our unique personal internal beliefs about reality. We can consciously work with our specific beliefs in order to create a new life. This means that our own words, thoughts, and emotions are the template of our future. It also means we are consciously co-creating reality to the degree we are aware of what is continuously happening within and around us. We are always creating something whether we are conscious of the mechanism or not. We can enrich the quality of what we manifest by being more Self-conscious. This requires greater awareness, and that comes from honestly seeing ourselves.

A useful way to focus on yourself is to look at your own inner balance. This is the balance between 'inner feminine' and 'inner masculine.' The masculine-feminine relationship has been discussed in all societies, religions, and cultures since the beginning of humanity. There is an intrinsic difference between what is masculine and feminine. By understanding those differences and appreciating the strengths of both, we can consciously use our inner masculine-feminine balance to be more effective in the physical world. Analyzing your masculine-feminine interplay helps you to take conscious steps to effectively balance your unique masculine and feminine qualities.

Humans love to mentally examine all things using three-dimensional physical logic. This helps the mind formulate new options and new actions. However, the actual answers more often come from the void, some place beyond definition. This book attempts to look at the mechanisms of the alliance between the masculine and feminine energies inside you and how these mechanisms affect your experience of life. Changes in manifestation begin by changing awareness of yourself and all that surrounds you. It is empowering to be able to mindfully see your own patterns and make new choices to act more consciously.

There is also value in looking at the external situation, your marriage or your love relationship, as a guide for better understanding of self. The principle of 'mirror-like wisdom' uses your love relationship to guide you to improve yourself. Your lover is always reflecting back to you some aspect of your own unseen self. Your lover can be your perfect teacher, if you are humble enough to learn from your lessons and wise enough to remain compassionate. It is challenging to begin the process of looking at your self. However, once you live from such an ongoing awareness, life gets much easier. As you become more fully conscious of your masculine and feminine aspects, you see how that balance changes in response to your daily challenges. It is all about being a better observer of yourself and acting more consciously.

More commonly, people project their pain on others. They blame their lovers and others for parts of themselves that have not yet healed. It seems easier to look beyond self for causes and answers. People often say, "If the world would change, then I would be safe." No. We must change ourselves and then our projected physical reality will change. By taking conscious steps to understand ourselves, we make better choices. This heals sub-conscious and unconscious places that have been invisibly controlling our physical manifestation. What we do not know about ourselves (sub-consciously and unconsciously) is what we are unconsciously bringing into manifestation in our lives. This includes our experience of our relationships, love, money, and the problems that we are so quick to blame on others.

For our happiness and highest good, our personal plans must be aligned with Source intention. 'Source' is the word I like best to describe the All, the Divine, God, or whatever word you might use to denote Higher Power. Otherwise, the object of our intention will be affected by our sub-conscious or unconscious beliefs, and will not manifest. It is critical that each soul has a way of knowing Source. There needs to be a way of validating our actions to see if they are in proper alignment. It is a challenge to look at yourself in a non-biased way. To know the world and to be able to function lovingly within it, we must first know self. That knowing combined with passionate desire is what brings clear manifestation into physical reality.

You can change your life by understanding how your own masculine and feminine aspects function together and by working with that balance. You can move into the flow of life by removing your own obstacles. As you understand more about the state of your masculine-feminine inner balance, you will see why some things haven't worked and why others have. You will understand how to consciously change from within to experience what is best for you. Increasing inner awareness is a powerful way to transform the illusion of victimization into personal power. Awareness is the key component.

This process is all about getting to know your Self (the part most connected to Source). After making connection to Self, you can work consciously with your inner feminine and masculine to change your life by attracting new people and experiences. It is as simple as learning the rules of manifestation and applying them for your desired outcome. The more you acknowledge that this is how manifestation works in your life, the more smoothly it will. You can begin to expect your world to manifest in new and more wonderful ways. You must also be willing to let go of the past so your new future can manifest.

I encourage you to use this book to look at yourself in a new way and to understand the real messages that you are sending out and are receiving back in manifested form. Once you fully unveil your personal sub-conscious and unconscious beliefs, you will be able to change them. Then, the world will also change based on intentions coming from your heart and from greater clarity. Extended periods of joy and Grace will follow.

This book is designed as a practical manual to help you better understand the interplay of the positive and negative masculine and the positive and negative feminine aspects operating within you and in other people in your life. After gaining an understanding of all four of these archetypes, you can begin to see how parts of yourself fit into each of those categories. This process gives you insight into how all these parts relate to each other and the world around you. This book shows you how to better understand yourself, your lover, family, friends, and anyone else in your life. You will learn how to change the dynamics of your relationships based on what you now see.

Joy is your birthright and can be the dominant emotional experience of your everyday life. This book shows you how to remove the obstacles that block your natural joyous flow. By doing the exercises you will increase your Self-awareness. You can then make the real life changes that are needed to be happier.

The next to last chapter entitled, 'Practical Exercises,' is dedicated to the details of the practical exercises that are interwoven throughout this book. I encourage you to do these exercises in the order they are given for at least three months. They will become an organic part of the way you see your Self and your world. You will learn that a useful way out of your pain is to look inside and change what you see through the lens of this new technique. Becoming conscious of your Self will gradually change everything in your life, until you become your true aware Self.

The Original Separation of Masculine and Feminine

Various myths from many cultures have a similar explanation for the puzzling situation of masculine and feminine separation. To simplify in a basic story form, the light of Source came to Earth and the light was the essence of human existence. In the very beginning, this light of human consciousness was whole and complete because it was still un-polarized. Then, it divided into two parts. Those two parts were 'Being' and 'Doing,' or you could say, feminine and masculine. The Bible says that Adam and Eve ate apples from the tree of life (good and evil polarities) and hence they "fell" from Wholeness. Humanity's goal has always been to regain the original Wholeness of the healthy integration of both. This can also be explained as re-connection to Source, something we all intuitively understand and yearn for.

What made the light of Source whole? The answer lies within its masculine and feminine parts. By understanding the parts, we understand how to re-integrate to become whole again. That is why it is essential to dive deeply into an active relationship with both your masculine and feminine sides. This blending of masculine and feminine is called the inner balance.

Humanity has 'fallen into polarity' and now it is time to 're-gain our Wholeness' once again. Source has separated into polarity, so that we each can better understand the individual aspects of pure feminine and pure masculine essences. Through this understanding, we can consciously return to a point of re-integration. This new Wholeness begins with healthy inner balance and can be personally retrieved through processes taught in this book.

We also need to keep in mind that there has been a negative masculine patriarchy ruling this planet throughout history. That is probably why it is called 'his-story.' This negative masculine force has dominated every human and still affects the collective consciousness. Societal roles for women have been directly affected by the negative masculine patriarchy. As a result, the fully natural positive feminine force has not been allowed to manifest yet. We have not yet seen the positive feminine power come to full expression even in cultures where women have been given more freedom, power, and equality.

At this time in history, it is important that the feminine come forth more purely because the folly of the negative masculine patriarchy is literally destroying Earth. To this end, it is extremely helpful to examine what it means to be healthy in your feminine Self, no matter whether you are physically a man or a woman. We all have both. Women need to own, accept, and properly use their masculine energy. Men need to own, accept, and properly use their feminine energy. This alone would change the world.

I strongly feel that the issue of labeling things as masculine and feminine is not about gender (men and women) and not about sexual orientation (gay or straight). Too many people have been wounded around their sexuality. It is a very raw subject because there is not enough good dialog about what is healthy and unhealthy regarding sexuality. Sexuality is constantly distorted into a marketing tool that lies about what is masculine and feminine. Many people are angry about these stereotypes, but nothing is changing. This book attempts to define the healthy masculine and feminine archetypes and to show how to use this insight to live a more potent life.

My message is that masculine and feminine energies are very different and both are essential to human survival and growth in consciousness. Both are to be honored and used together to accomplish goals. If you find yourself in emotional reaction to the use of the terms 'masculine' and 'feminine' in this text, please allow yourself to set aside old biases and look deeper at the intended meaning of what is being expressed. Remember, there is a positive and negative side to both masculine and feminine energies. We have all experienced these archetypes in our relationships with others. By being more conscious of the patterns that are being played out in your life, you can consciously create your future.

This book will carefully define the aspects of the four major archetypes, the positive and negative masculine, and the positive and negative feminine. Understanding these aspects and the paradigms that arise from them will allow you to watch others and yourself using this method. These new insights will allow you to more consciously act in your life to manifest more simplicity and success. The purpose of clearly defining these archetypes is to bring the balanced halves back together into Wholeness. We are literally rejoining masculine and feminine energies. Once they are working together, a force bigger than both is created. Perfected inner balance is Wholeness.

The beginning of Wholeness is usually first found on the inner level through a healthy inner balance. The next step is to move that balance out of Self to improve your life. Your love relationship is the most profound externalization of your inner balance. It is the arena in which you are constantly reflected back to yourself through your experiences with your lover or partner. The process is instant. If the connection is clear with your lover, you can literally generate a new energy that is bigger than either of you and that energy feeds back into both of you until you both experience a huge amplification of life force energy.

If the external union is attempted before the fuller inner balance is established, it will not be as easy. The condition of the inner balance is the inner template of your externalized physical love relationship. Therefore, if you find a new love relationship before you have worked on your own issues, you are most likely to attract a lover who is probably at the same level of balance or imbalance as you are. This can be fine, if both of you work together on inner balance. It is wise to be this aware of your relationships and this book gives you very specific ways to watch and change your relationships.

Seeing Within Self

Seeing within is the act of being the Observer and the Actor simultaneously. Observation is the key to realization and eventual transformation. Everything you need to know about yourself is all there all the time. Our patterns are usually repetitive and accessible by our own consciousness. A commitment to introspection and self-analysis can lead to transformation. As you improve at observing yourself, you will be able to stop yourself before you act unconsciously. Source will let you know, if you are willing to listen. It takes daily practice to center your mind in a way that allows the intuition to come forth into your active mind. The process of seeing within must be practiced both mentally and intuitively. The intuitive seeing must come from the silence (the void) which connects clearly to Source, while mental seeing uses the Observer mind to know Self as it lives within each of us.

Seeing within shows you how your inner balance changes from moment to moment. The interplay between your masculine and feminine aspects is a dance in which, ideally, your masculine and feminine share the lead. This dance is a beautiful exchange between Being and Doing. It is a flow between the two and yet it is both at once and, at any one moment, it is more of one than the other. We can consciously watch and understand how circumstances propel us into a changing inner balance. Once you understand this mechanism, you can make conscious choices to change your actions mid-stream and create a reality more in alignment with Source consciousness.

Begin by watching yourself throughout the day. Are you able to act and simultaneously watch each action? Are you also able to interpret and judge your actions as you continue to act? This is a lot at first, but with continued practice, it is possible to remain in Observer mode continuously. Your critical voice usually comments back to you when you look in the mirror. You can become the literal mirror of yourself and you must observe with compassion. The essential element is compassion. You must be honest and kind towards yourself. It is helpful to see your 'weaknesses' truly as a lack of understanding. Then you can use that information to make positive future choices.

Remember that there are "no regrets" and, therefore, there is no guilt. Regrets take us backward into the past in a destructive way, because we are not able to change the past. When we have regrets, we set ourselves up to fail every time. Once you see your previous 'faults' as a lack of understanding, then you have the opportunity to make new choices to create a better life. Be gentle with yourself as you look deeply inside. There have been no mistakes along your path and everything you did has led to this moment. Allow gratitude toward yourself to replace any doubts or regrets about your journey through life.

Let's begin the seeing within process by examining what can be considered the negative aspects of masculine behavior (irrespective of gender or sexual orientation):

NEGATIVE OVERACTIVE MASCULINE BEHAVIORS:

Arrogance
Pride
Self-Righteousness
Control
Violence
Bigotry
Rage
Anger
Impatience
Pushiness
Denigration
Dominance

Abusiveness
Impulsiveness
Loudness
Mental manipulation
Obsession
Ego domination
Lust
Greed
Selfishness
Revenge
Aggressiveness

NEGATIVE UNDERACTIVE MASCULINE BEHAVIORS:

Confusion
Weakness
Unfocused
Shyness
Inactive
Laziness
Indecisiveness
Weak-willed
Procrastination
Sloppiness
Tardiness
Uncertainty
Egoless
Passive aggression
Bitterness
Guilt
Fearfulness
Regret
Hopelessness
Ungroundedness

As you can see, either too much masculine forcefulness or too little presence is problematic. By watching for the emotions or feeling-qualities listed above, you begin to see whether your masculine orientation is more dominant or subdued. At a deeper level, you can look to see what life circumstances bring out the negative attributes listed above. As you observe yourself, write down the circumstance and write down the emotional reaction you had to that event. After doing this for a while, you will begin to see patterns of stimulus and response. The last step will be to consciously alter your responses in the moment that the next stimulus appears. This is a valuable way to change. Remember to do this compassionately. If you want others to treat you respectfully, you must begin by doing the same for yourself. (You may want to refer to your notes when you begin the Practical Exercises later in this book.)

Here is a list of some negative emotional states or behaviors generally considered common to the feminine (irrespective of gender or sexual orientation):

NEGATIVE OVERACTIVE FEMININE BEHAVIORS:

Obsession
Complaining
Suffering
Emotional manipulation
Pouting
Controlling
Moodiness
Ego
Vanity
Pride
Gluttony
Flirting
Teasing

Cattiness
Overwhelmed
Revengeful
Gossipy
Self-indulgent

NEGATIVE UNDERACTIVE FEMININE BEHAVIOR:

Depression
Grief
Despair
Laziness
Weakness
Confusion
Inactivity
Lack of boundaries
Escapism
Emotionless
Emptiness
Fearfulness
Ungrounded
Indecisive
Overly sensitive
Insecure
Fearful
Terrorized
Immobilized

Placing a quality into one category is difficult, as is defining it as specifically 'negative.' What is distinctly 'masculine' and what is distinctly 'feminine' is also a hard question. There are not black-and-white answers. Establishing balance is the key. It is helpful to think of all these emotional and active states on a scale of polarity. For example, in looking at the extremes of victimization and control, there is a middle ground and there are many shades of gray between the extremes. When looking at human qualities (such as those listed above), try to define the polarities that relate to that specific emotion. By understanding the polarities it is easier to see all the conditions that lie between the extremes. For example, victimization/control, power/fear, love/hate, being/doing, and so on. These polarities represent all the different extremes that humans need to balance.

Feminine Energy

The essence of feminine energy has not changed throughout history. Women of all cultures share common activities such as childbirth, child care, gardening, food preparation, education of children, clothing the family, and maintaining the home. These duties are based on the feminine qualities of love, nurturance, creativity, and emotional sensitivity. But this is only the basic material level of the feminine energy in action.

The simplest way to start talking about the feminine is by talking about Being. Being is a state of stillness and stillness is the place of silence that opens to Source guidance. The experience of Being is richly filled with the treasures of love, understanding, compassion, gratitude, forgiveness, humility, connection to Source, trust, nurturing, emotional support, Grace, and so much more. Being is often unnoticed in societies that value materialism. The patriarchy, which currently exemplifies more of the negative masculine, denigrates those who are not big money makers or power brokers. The finer qualities of feminine energy are not honored.

Our society has lied to us about the greater values of Being, as well as the potential of positive feminine energy to change the world. Culture does change, but the essence of the positive feminine continues steadfastly through time. If people can begin to fully experience the true essence of femininity in these increasingly open times, it will be possible for individuals to establish a deeper inner balance and a stronger personal and collective outer manifestation of Wholeness on Earth.

The positive feminine energy, for both men and women, is about holding space in a way that allows Source inspiration to be consciously brought into action. It is about listening in silence to Source.

What is heard in that quiet space is the essence of what is yet to be created in physical form. The positive feminine is all about receiving Truth from Source and knowing what is to be brought forth into your life. The positive masculine energy is the force that is needed to manifest what the feminine knows. Men influenced by the negative masculine manifest negative things. A man who lives apart from his feminine Being does not hear Source and therefore, does not manifest a life in tune with Source consciousness.

The positive feminine knows. She sees the beauty that can come, but doesn't necessarily know how to bring that beauty into manifestation. The feminine needs her positive masculine to manifest any reality. She could clearly know the truest message directly from Source, but without an ability to translate that into physical action, she may remain a knower and not a doer. Strong emotions (conscious, subconscious, and unconscious) often immobilize action. Emotions must be worked with consciously and released to keep the channel of manifestation (positive masculine) open. If emotions are denied or remain unacknowledged, the feminine becomes clogged and unable to access Source guidance.

The positive feminine is the nurturer, mother, lover, and the one who cares. Only because she is in tune with her own emotions, is she able to be sensitive to others. When she is led by her intuition, she can be compassionate, sensitive, and nurturing. Feelings lead to caring. Caring is love and that love magnetizes even more love. Wonderful acts bring more gratitude and they attract greater prosperity. More prosperity brings loads of generosity and that generosity can feed the poor. Being finally translates into real live manifestation. The Being part of Self is most intimately connected with our personal inner template of manifestation.

Feminine energy is also the emotional part of Self. Emotions are the language of the heart. We must be in touch with our positive feminine in order to be aware of ourselves fully. By staying in touch with our emotions, our actions will stay true to our hearts. Actions coming from an honest emotional place produce more balanced results and more compassion. Without awareness of the positive feminine, we get stuck on some negative masculine head trip leading only as far as our ego can see. We must constantly see the bigger picture. We must live by what we know from our direct Observation of what our inner masculine and feminine are producing. This is always what we are seeing right there in front of ourselves.

There is something very organic about the positive feminine. It's a feeling of realness or peace that comes from 'knowing by Being.' It is called resonance, a state of Grace that exists because all of your obstructions have been removed. Everything is truly in correct alignment. You simply have to 'get out of your own way' and allow perfection to blossom because you are no longer interfering. Use your feminine feeling-self to get to know yourself until you really see who you are. Once you feel that organic blissful knowingness, then you will always demand that quality of life. From there, the quality of your life will begin to naturally improve.

The positive feminine acts as a container. She is a container for the masculine at conception and a container for the baby during pregnancy. She is a safe place for things to grow. Those are the obvious container roles. Let's look a little deeper. How does Mom deal with the situation when her baby is raging out of control because he just dropped his bottle? Is the feminine containing that moment as well? Is she holding space and allowing drama to pass? This is where the stillness of the depth of the well of the positive feminine literally holds space by not reacting, so that drama can pass at its own pace. This requires emotional maturity and strength.

The positive feminine is creative, artistic, sensual, colorful, playful, and fresh. Costumes, dances, festivals, and parties have been hosted by amazing females of every era. Fairy tales and costume balls are some of the finest manifestations of the imagination of the positive feminine. The positive feminine is the true source of creativity and is the force that brings new evolution and positive change to our lives. Those who carry the color and diversity of life itself must be honored.

All of these feminine qualities live within each man and woman, to some extent. It is to your advantage to look inside and see how your feminine is working for you. Discover how she can live through you in a more effective way. The same process will be reiterated after the masculine section, and then, careful attention should be placed on how your masculine and feminine relate. Success in life is greatly dependent on the balance of your inner masculine and feminine and how they play out in your world.

Emotions are the cornerstone of feminine energy. Emotions are likened to water, and like water, they easily change form very quickly. Water is not a stable element. It transforms from vapor to liquid to ice and back again, swiftly. The same mutability is true of natural feminine energy if it is not balanced with a positive masculine energy. The positive masculine force stabilizes the mutability of emotions. Mutability is the strength of the positive feminine to connect to Source and to other people.

When unobstructed by pain, emotions connect more fully than ever through the heart to open to the deepest part of the soul. This full-on connection produces the sensation called ecstasy. It is this experience of the purest essence of the love in your heart, which opens you to savor the nectar of Source. This connection is amplified as old painful emotions are gradually transmuted into calm silence. In silence, Source speaks clearly and the positive masculine responds with balanced action or non-action. Being that is connected to Source assures clarity of action. The emphasis must be on Being.

Emotions stir from the deepest place, if we create the space to allow them. Authentic quiet space is needed to hear Source. Painful emotions must heal in order to create a quiet space for new intuitive insights. Painful emotions must be consciously acknowledged and brought to the surface to be processed, and not just dismissed. These uncomfortable emotions can be processed out of the body over time. The list of possible therapies and modalities that can assist you in this process is long. The true core of most of these therapies is self-awareness. Your Observer Self steps in here. Your Observer Self stays aware of your emotional body and your emotional expression or non-expression. Your Observer can show you a way to release painful emotions. It also may guide you to postpone processing until you can be in a supportive environment. If you can learn to stay in the present and listen to your own Observer, you will always know what to do.

Remember that emotions are highly mutable and that painful feelings change quickly if you give them a little space and time. When you let emotions rise to the surface and be expressed, they quickly move away and new realities emerge. The key is not to get stuck or to fixate on any one emotional state. If you give the swirling emotion some time to unwind, it will, and peace returns. When you try to stop this process, you get stuck in pushing against what could have been a transient moment if the emotions were simply allowed. Be patient in this way. If you feel a wave of crazy emotion rising within, let yourself feel it and let it move through you with sound and motion. If you try to analyze it or stop it, you will break the natural flow and it is likely you will continue to experience emotional pain until you get the deeper emotional message.

Though we want emotions to be revealed and to move, emotions make bad masters. Since emotion, like water, is so mutable, it makes a poor director of your life. Yet, unresolved emotion held in the subconscious is the director until deeper emotional healing occurs. After the painful emotions have been processed, the "waters become still." At this point you can act, instead of reacting from unresolved pain. Source then becomes the new director and manifestation comes from the stillness instead of the storm, improving the quality of life. Stilling inner water (clearing painful emotions) is important work for healing the wounded feminine.

As an example, let's say Jane was deeply terrorized by her two brothers throughout her teenage years. Jane is now thirty-five years old and has two of her own daughters that she raises using harsh discipline. She screams at them and criticizes them frequently. Jane is not tender or nurturing to anyone. If we look at Jane's behavior using inner balance analysis, we see that Jane seems to be unconscious of holding onto and operating from the unexpressed terror of her teenage years. She is unaware of her wounded feminine. Therefore, in response to feeling out of control or unsafe, Jane's negative masculine comes out in a very angry way. If Jane inadvertently allows herself to sink down into her positive feminine, she feels the terror, panics, and represses again, and usually retracts back to the negative masculine. The only way Jane will find a way out of the pain is by feeling her feelings of terror and finding a way to release these feelings from her sub-conscious. As long as Jane simply remains angry, she will be postponing her healing.

It is important to clear negative emotion, as emotions are the foundation of manifestation. Emotions are the original building blocks of "thought forms." Thought forms are most effective when they are consciously imbued with focused amounts of passionate emotion (intention). Highly charged thought forms are most likely to manifest in physical form. In other words, when you want something to come into your life, you need to focus on that thing and get very emotionally excited about it. Repetition and consistency are keys to successful lasting manifestation. This 'passionate template' is the secret of manifestation and focused emotion (passion) is the driving force. The positive masculine aspect provides the focus. The positive feminine provides the motivating emotion. Working together, healthy manifestation occurs.

The Dark Feminine

Perhaps it seems easier to read only about the beauty of the feminine and just reverse each of the positive aspects to find the 'dark,' as in 'negative feminine.' However, the negative feminine deserves some real attention. We can aid in our own healing by learning how to identify the dark aspects of our feminine nature. By seeing our imbalances, we can take conscious steps to change our ways. It is helpful to remember that too little and too much of any aspect of human expression brings imbalance.

Let's start with the basic issue of emotionality since that is the cornerstone of femininity. Balanced emotionality is essential for intuition to be heard.

If the emotions are completely absent externally, then something is out of balance on the inside (negative feminine). The lack of balance is usually caused by pain that has not been acknowledged or released from the body. It is common in this case for the wounded person to operate out of their negative masculine aspect. If pain caused by the unexpressed negative feminine begins to be felt, the focus can shift immediately back to the masculine. This is a protective maneuver, a form of escapism and a way out of pain (negative feminine) by moving into action (negative masculine). These types are classic workaholics (negative masculine) or often very mental (negative feminine) people. They are outwardly flat and inwardly they are emotionally volatile. Their "corks blow" at a regular frequency and then they become quiet. This peace lasts for a little while until another cycle repeats and they blow up again.

The opposite archetype is the overly externally emotional type (negative feminine). We know these types of people. They are the ones who are overly emotional. They never get anything done because they're consumed by crying, screaming or complaining. They especially like to tell everyone the details of how they were last victimized. The sad story sounds pathetic after the third time you hear it. These people are consumed by their wounded emotions. They actually become the emotions they are feeling. Their physical bodies change to show the emotions that they have held for so long. Their masculine energy is drowned by excessive water of old painful emotion until they become ineffective in life. Finally, they become so powerless that other people have to care for them.

Up to this point, we have been generalizing about too much and too little emotionality. Now let us look at some specific examples of the negative feminine. We will begin with gossip. Gossip is an example of the blending of the negative feminine with the externalized negative masculine. Gossipers usually have low self-esteem. They gossip to feel better about themselves. If they can find something 'worse' in other people, then they can live out their own repressed emotions through these other people's stories. Gossipers also deflect others' awareness away from themselves (the gossiper) by pointing attention elsewhere. The problem is that what they focus upon increases, so they end up bringing more negativity into their own lives by only seeing the suffering of others. Low self-esteem issues are often directly connected with the issue of gossip.

Dreamers are another group to consider. These people have strong intuitive abilities and therefore prefer to live in the inner worlds. They are very inspired and creative people, but they do not usually function well in society. They can not understand much about responsibility or the structure of life itself. They get excited about their next vision but are unable to physically manifest those visions into real action. Dreamers are considered weak for this reason. They usually know that they are different and withdraw socially. This isolates them further and drives them deeper into the dreaming.

Self-indulgence and selfishness are unattractive character traits. These are feminine forms of negative ego. For example, "I am the Queen and the world truly does revolve around me." Remember that the Queen can be either a man or a woman and either gay or straight. The essence of the negative ego is to selfishly ignore the needs of others. These types are not able to see themselves through the eyes of others, so they have no real sense of Self. Without the mirror-like wisdom of honest personal reflection, the ego resorts to manifesting the ideals of society which are grossly out of balance.

Overly-caring selfless hero-type people are also annoying. These are the ones that invade your personal space. They need to know all the ugly details about everything and they especially obsess on everybody's drama. Emotional drama feeds them. They usually want to know what more they can do and ask the details of how they can do the job best. It all seems very innocent, but it is terribly co-dependant. They start having a bad day if you are having a bad day. They lack positive masculine energy. They are busy trying to fix people who they have no reason to be dealing with in the first place. These wounded heroes have unacknowledged internal emotional pain. They focus their emotions and thoughts on other people's difficulties to avoid feeling their own pain. The point is that they need to shift their focus back to Self in order to heal.

Victims are people that deal with their own pain by blaming someone else or some situation for their problems. In this case, the negative feminine is operating, causing the person to feel they have no power and that they are "a victim of circumstances beyond their control." Once anyone admits they are powerless, they are. Intention is directed by unconscious and subconscious beliefs that make up the internal template (inner balance). The essence of the feeling of being helpless to victimizers literally sets the unconscious signal to attract more victimization. This painful manifestation continues to increase in intensity until one finally sees the inner cause. People that believe that they are victims actually manifest real victimizers to prove their own beliefs to themselves. This is a dangerous template to hold because it truly makes people vulnerable to negativity.

People who are primarily fear-based are very similar to the victim type. The fear template literally attracts situations and people that are going to cause them to feel fear. Life is always striving for perfect balance and this is no exception. The best way to heal is to feel the painful places in your psyche in order to release the pain that resides there. In other words, the way out of pain is into it. If the way out of the pain is to feel it, then Source will provide opportunities to trigger or activate unacknowledged emotions. Hence, fearful people attract more victimization in order to feel the pain of fear so that they can cry or shake it from their bodies.

Masculine Energy

Masculine energy is the other half of Wholeness. It has been the dominant energy controlling Earth since we can first remember. The true nature of masculine energy is to positively direct, plan, and act in order to bring thought into physical manifestation. Masculine energy is the Doing force that sets the course, the rules of engagement, and the expectations for certain outcomes. All of this requires the left half of the brain, linear thinking, and mental focus. Therefore, manifestation is directed by masculine energy. This is important because we need food to eat and we need to build homes for protection. Without taking action, we eventually die. This is the strength of the healthy masculine. Masculine energy provides stability through actions connected to Source guidance.

The masculine force is projected force. The push outward beyond self is often goal-oriented with nothing other than an objective in mind. In this way, masculine energy can be very narrow-minded, often missing the bigger picture. Masculine energy is not the realm of the imagination or creativity. It is the force that moves intention into action and manifestation. Using focused masculine energy is essential to living a successful life.

Masculine energy has the ability to disregard pain and emotions during the task at hand. In times of battle or during the hunt, masculine energy doesn't get distracted. Having an emotional breakdown or crying on the battlefield could easily cause your own death. Positive masculine energy is needed to focus on the task at hand in the immediate present so that you can take appropriate action. Focus is the driving force that is needed to complete certain tasks and to accomplish planned goals. Masculine energy is the completing force that follows through and gets things done properly. Without positive masculine energy present, there is often emotional chaos (negative feminine).

Masculine energy is the planner, architect, and builder. The initial creative vision comes from the positive feminine in communication with Source. However, the detailed plan of manifestation is put into place by positive masculine energy. Calculation based on observation needs to be combined with intuition (positive feminine) to result in appropriate action. This requires focus, intuition, and determination. The challenge is to always stay open to positive feminine energy for inspiration and intuition in order to alter your course as needed. This requires humility and flexibility. When all of these qualities come together, healthy manifestation occurs.

Our age-old problem is that the negative masculine has been overrated, overplayed, and given too much power on this planet for too long without proper blending with the healthy feminine. It's been action without introspection or inspiration. Earth has historically functioned using severity without mercy, and this is the wrong use of Will. We must bring Source into manifestation within ourselves and into our world. It is necessary for both the healthy masculine and feminine halves to come together to form Wholeness. Balancing our individual inner templates will transform our lives by bringing forth healthier external manifestation.

The healthy masculine listens to his own connection to Source (positive feminine) and he does what he is directed to do (positive masculine). "Love is the Law, Love under Will." Love is positive feminine and is the very nectar of Source. Will is the driving force (positive masculine) which manifests pure intention from Source into beauty on Earth. It really has nothing to do with the personal ego. Masculine energy is the vehicle to manifest Source intelligence on Earth for the benefit of all beings. The feminine needs to be ever-present to offer guidance. That is why the positive masculine listens to the positive feminine within, and she receives guidance directly from Source.

If we are not the conduit of Source, then our ego is controlling manifestation. This is an important distinction. Source gives us personal will and yet our job is to align that individual will with Source Will to uplift ourselves and our world to greater Wholeness. Our negative masculine must be tempered, yet the masculine itself must not be abolished. It can be tempered by the positive feminine. This requires appreciation, compassion, forgiveness, humility, understanding, and valor, to be used together to transcend the historical patriarchy (negative masculine). That transmutation is a difficult task for masculine expression trained in the old negative masculine world. There are as of yet few models for positive masculine energy in the world today. Therefore, the answers lie within your Self and must be sought there.

More and more, people are honoring their inner feminine energy. We are beginning to see leaders with more emotional sensitivity, compassion, and even a touch of Grace. The world is changing and masculine energy is integrating with feminine to create in a more sane and balanced way. This is still an individual process. We need more people with positive masculinity to come forth and show others how to bring out their healthy feminine expression. As more and more balanced humans come fully into action, humanity will begin to see the new integrated consciousness as normal. Then, society will have more positive role models. It is time for these changes now. Let the pioneers of consciousness come forth and inspire the masses to be more positive.

Presence of mind is the backbone of masculine energy. A clear and focused mind (positive masculine) is an essential component of traditional masculine activities such as hunting, putting away the harvest, providing protection, providing shelter, planning and procreation. Mindfulness is not just about showing up mentally, it is also about manifesting inner plans into action in the material world. A healthy masculine exhibits an ability to persistently move towards specific goals while keenly observing what is happening around him in every moment. The positive masculine is about staying with the task at hand until it is complete while not being distracted by random thoughts.

This requires allowing the mind to be able to move into Observer mode, while simultaneously acting consciously as the Doer. It is critical to keep the masculine projective and the feminine intuitive working together at the same time. Imagine being on stage with a mini-speaker in your ear. The guy behind the curtain is hooked into a huge computer and is ready to put any answer you need into your ear at the exact moment you need the information. That is how Source can speak directly to your personal mind. The personal will (positive masculine) can manifest anything, if it only listens to Source.

A balanced mind comes through balancing your inner masculine and feminine. The healthy feminine receptive ability draws the needed guidance from Source and the healthy masculine turns those inspirations into real physical expressions. The entire process requires organization and structure. It needs constant vigilance on the task at hand and on the original goal. Acquiring these skills usually takes considerable and consistent practice over many years.

Masculine action begins with an awareness (positive feminine) of what is needed. For instance, "We need food," or "we need shelter." In this case, the elders assemble to determine the needs of the tribe, or a community to access needs of their neighborhood. If it is water that is needed, a plan is formulated to build a community water system. This includes a plan for construction, a list of materials, and the estimation of the amount of human labor that is required. It also comes with a price tag and the re-payment plan must also be clarified.

The components (labor, materials, design templates, and money) are assembled and work begins. The monitoring of work also begins and plans change, on site, until the objectives of the plan are met and the project is complete. The steps of the process can be outlined (see below). Understanding this process is important because this is exactly how healthy masculine expression works in order to accomplish anything, in any context, with every project. You could be watering the grass, helping your child, or building a bridge, it all works in the same way in the following order:

1. Remain in a state of **awareness**
2. Define the **needs** in present time
3. Form a plan of **action**
4. Form a plan of **re-payment**
5. Assemble the **components**
6. **Begin** construction/operation of the project
7. **Monitor** the progress of the project
8. **Change** the course of action as needed
9. Determine when the project is **complete**
10. **Move on** to the next most important project

If you are using this sequence of thinking, you are well on your way to using your mind more effectively to accomplish your goals. This requires focus and consistency because the mind tends to wander. The mind mostly tends to think about the past and the future. The healthy masculine process requires that your mind completely focus on the present and not past or future. This takes strict discipline to watch yourself carefully. Again, it is the Observer who watches the mind to make sure you stay only in present time. It could take months or years of daily practice to master this ability. Watch yourself when stress comes and see whether you remain centered in present time. If you start to slip away into another time, consciously pull yourself back into the present.

Positive masculine energy can be thought of as 'the guardian of body and soul.' The keenness of the mind and the instant ability to assimilate what the intuition (positive feminine) is saying are at the core of the positive masculine as it obtains inner balance. Your positive masculine Self is ever-present in your life. As you listen and follow accordingly, you are protected by your guardian Self (positive masculine). A calm mind (positive masculine) opens awareness to all that is around. Less distractions lead to more focus. Focus moves you toward your goals. Don't get distracted. Focus on staying in present time. Try it at home and throughout your life. Stop yourself at any moment and ask yourself if you are focused on what is happening around you, in your immediate environment in that moment. See how long you can consciously continue this practice in order to increase positive masculine potency.

Potency is a great word because it really speaks about reserve energy. We need reserve energy to confront unexpected challenges. It is essential particularly for the positive masculine to hold extra energy for the protection of self and others. The Observer Self can monitor how much reserve is present. How does energy leak out of your life? Holding painful emotions obviously drains core vital energy. Overwork and lack of sleep directly diminish your reserve. Substances including sugar, caffeine, nicotine, drugs, and artificial foods seriously deplete your energy system. Potency must be preserved by remaining self-aware and by acting accordingly.

Ethics is an important part of positive masculine energy. Ethics is action based on awareness of other people, the larger community, and the entire planet. It is another big job for the Observer. Situations need to be monitored while ethical evaluations are made and changes in action are simultaneously altered. A healthy inner balance requires a feeling for the emotional tone of situations and how they can be translated through the masculine mind into ethical action. Ethics requires an ability to access Source information (positive feminine) and bring that knowingness into manifestation (positive masculine).

It is helpful to monitor all of these masculine qualities within yourself and in others. The masculine manifestation process seems to pivot around the basic masculine mental process (outlined earlier in this chapter). Understanding the manifestation process and how it can be used to make things happen is very useful. Watch how you use your mind to deal with the events of each day. Listen for Source information and simultaneously translate that guidance into action. If enough individuals lived this way, society would change profoundly.

The Dark Masculine

The primary characteristic of the masculine energy is mind. In the case of the dark masculine, we need to explore the extremes of too much or too little mental function. In the case of too much mental activity, the principal effect is lack of acknowledgment of emotionality (the feminine). Therefore, the feminine aspect does not function positively. A lack of intuitional ability leads to manifestation that is not in alignment with Source. An unbalanced person manifests situations that are difficult because their inner template is out of balance. Mental types obsess over things to the point of insomnia or possibly even mental illness. It is not easy to be around these types because they are usually very intense. They talk a lot and are nervous about most things. They tend to wander off into fantasies about the future and tend to compare what is currently happening to past events. They rarely can honestly answer the question, "How are you feeling right now?"

The opposite situation occurs when someone has too little mental activity. As you can imagine, this is much like the dreamer type we examined in the Dark Feminine chapter. However, in this case there is ineffective or non-existent masculine mental energy. Because the negative masculine is weak and ineffective, the quality of life defaults to whatever feminine abilities exist. Since the mind is the key to positive masculine energy, the masculine is ineffective when the mind doesn't work well. Without the positive masculine operating, the feminine side is unprotected and often reverts to the negative feminine.

Greed is one way the selfish negative masculine expresses itself. It's all about "What I want… What I want to have for me…I never seem to have enough…I'm never satisfied…I need more." Greed is an outward expression of the hunger to fill the emptiness of a wounded soul. Specific emotional wounds stimulate greed for something that will supposedly make the pain go away. Since this never works, the greed continues and the person's focus moves on to the next object or goal state. This activity is a product of a mind cut off from Source.

Lust is another dark masculine trait. In this case, the negative masculine is focusing sexually in an unhealthy way, looking to impose itself or conquer another in order to feel powerful. This is a negative focus because it is a distraction from the balance intended between the positive feminine and positive masculine selves. The underlying emotional pain is being avoided by re-focusing on sexuality in a negative way. Lust is usually associated with desiring what is illicit, secret, and ultimately unattainable. Unconscious actions result when the genuine connection to Source is ignored. Lust is often used as a distraction from pain.

Anger is a very common negative masculine trait. It is present in all of us irrespective of gender. It is usually one of the most superficial emotional layers. Sometimes anger must be released through some form of processing before you are able to go into the deeper emotional layers. The presence of anger can be used as an indicator of the necessity to feel more deeply within for the real emotional truth. In any case, anger must be worked with consciously or there is a danger others may be hurt.

For example, let's say Jane is embarrassed by her friend who has made a comment about Jane's clothing. Jane is actually fearful, is self-conscious, and has low self-esteem. However, on the surface, she is reactive and angry after hearing the comments. Jane's most superficial layer is anger. When you challenge her, she snaps back. This is a coping mechanism. This is the way she keeps 'dangerous people' away. So, whenever we encounter anger within ourselves or in others, we need to look within for the deeper core layer that is really driving the more superficial anger.

Arrogance and pride are manifestations of negative masculine ego that are often pointers to low self-esteem. This negative masculine type routinely puts on a big, self-righteous show to distract from vulnerabilities that lie deeper within. The negative masculine is more problematic than the negative feminine because the very nature of masculine energy is to project out, which affects other people, whereas feminine energy reflects back on self. Arrogance causes loss of the intuitive connection to Source and results in a masculine which, without feminine input, is bound to create an unbalanced life.

Gluttony is a symptom that screams, "I can't get enough!" A person with this aspect of the negative masculine feels as though there is a big hole to fill. The pain comes from what seems to be missing, and that is the confusion. The deeper truth is that no 'thing' ever brings joy. Some of the wealthiest people in the world have the worst problems with gluttony. They have lost touch with their sensitive positive feminine selves. They don't care about anyone but themselves. They want it all and they do not care who they hurt to get it.

It is essential to continually look deeply into the masculine self to identify when these dark characteristics come forth in your inner dialog and in your dealings with other people. If you can catch yourself moving into these negative places, you then have the opportunity to make choices to re-direct your actions. The key is to catch yourself before acting unconsciously. This is the art of making mid-course corrections using your Observer Self. This is the positive masculine working in an effective way to improve the quality of life. Keep watching yourself and keep moving closer to what you know as Source. Use the positive feminine to guide you.

Feminine Nectar

Nectar is a refined and concentrated substance that holds the potency of the being who secretes it. On a physical level, it is sap dripping from a tree or the fine pollen that is formed inside flowers to attract bees. The positive feminine energy literally oozes its nectar into the world for those who have the eyes to see, the tongue to taste, and the nose to appreciate it. We are talking about the sensual and secret aspects of the positive feminine. We have already discussed the characteristics that define the true nature of positive feminine energy. Nectar is the actual manifestation that comes from the balanced healthy feminine. Emptiness is the foundation of nectar production.

Emptiness is the fertile environment that most allows clear connection to Source. Clearing the emotional pain and misunderstandings from within brings emptiness into consciousness. This quiet empty space is the portal for plugging into awareness of Source. However, it takes more than emptiness to produce nectar. Love and intention are the other two ingredients. Nectar is materialized love. Nectar is only produced in the presence of strong feelings of love. The obvious example is that people produce juices and fragrances while making love. Flowers release pollen to attract bees to spread their sexual nectar to other plants. For humans, the key is to become so stimulated by love that you produce your own nectar. This occurs during the state of ecstasy and that is the purest core of the positive feminine energy. If you are able to experience emptiness and stoke the fires of sensual passion using love, then you are ready to apply the intention needed to produce nectar.

The intention part is quite easy. It requires asking Source with repetition and consistency for manifestation that is in alignment with the values of Source (Love). This concept is summarized in the following quote, "Love is the Law, Love under Will." In other words, Love is the Law of the Universe, Love that is manifested in balance with the Will of Source. When your individual conscious intention aligns with love in this way, anything can manifest. It takes the positive feminine to do any of this.

The most challenging part of this process is being able to experience states of ecstasy for longer and longer periods of time. This is the key to higher mastery. To accomplish this, all of our basic needs must first be met. It is harder to maintain a sustained state of ecstasy while fighting on a battlefield or while starving. It requires setting aside some quiet private time after all of your emotional and physical needs have been met.

Healthy sexuality is the closest thing humans have to experiencing higher dimensional reality and ecstasy. This is where healthy sexuality and inner balance merge. The fullest experience of healthy sexuality can not be enjoyed until the inner feminine and masculine are balanced in both partners. Once this inner balance is attained, full-on healthy sexual practice is beyond description. This type of expanded sexuality can be sustained for many hours during one lovemaking session. It is like upgrading your energy system from a steam engine (three-dimensional) to a nuclear reactor (multi-dimensional). Your brain starts to function differently after it has been infused with this 'liquid nectar of ecstasy.' You can feel currents of electromagnetic energy rushing throughout your entire Being and your awareness of Source consciousness increases.

You can more effectively maintain this feeling of sexual expansion if you have first practiced inner balance. The peace of mind and centeredness of a perfected inner balance is a source of pleasure because you are able to share your nectar sexually with another person who also cares about expanded consciousness. Moving inner balance equilibrium into healthy sexuality increases the vitality of your entire essence and connects you more fully to Source.

There are many wonderful books and DVDs for sale on the Internet to teach advanced sexual practice. I encourage you to study these materials and incorporate them into your daily life. If you do the inner work first, you will attract a more balanced partner because you always attract from the current level of clarity of your internal template. Inner balancing will attract more conscious people and situations into your life. You will also naturally attract people who are humble and willing to be honest about themselves, because this is what you are doing. Your life becomes easier as you understand how to function from a balanced inner place.

Nectar expresses itself in many forms other than sexual ecstasy. Nectar is love in action. It could be as simple as looking into someone's eyes. Love can be conveyed in simple ways, such as deeply listening to someone's story or just by brushing the hair out of a child's face. Acting from an inner place filled with the nectar of love is extremely powerful. If you walk into a room filled with people and you are truly in the consciousness of love, people will respond to you with more love. It is that simple. If you are in this state, you are fully present (positive feminine) with love and will know exactly how to respond to those around you. This is how to be truly present. This quality of presence only comes after years of self-growth, clarity of heart, and clarity of purpose. This is the experience of the state of Grace.

There are many other ways to share your nectar. Selfless service and humanitarian acts are obvious ways to help bring new consciousness to others without imposing dogma. Loving other people is about sharing love and not about promoting any story or belief system. Selfless service is just about loving and helping others in meaningful ways without expecting anything in return. It is not about directly teaching others about this inner balance analysis; it is about living your balance by putting other people's needs ahead of your own at certain times. It is true that you must first take great emotional care of yourself before you extend love and support to others. Once your 'cup is full,' the natural next step is to share your nectar with others. The simple objective is to treat other people consciously.

Keep focused on feeling your own state of ecstasy so that you have a richer life and you will continue to have an abundance of nectar to share. Be discriminating with whom you share your nectar. If you are conscious enough to experience regular states of ecstasy, then you are wise enough to know where others around you sit in consciousness. Surround yourself with people of love. Create a new world right now based on your expanded awareness of life. Bring only those who also cherish the ideal of conscious love into your inner circle. Always be aware of who you are and how you are being reflected by those around you. Align your consciousness with Source and act from that place of increased clarity.

A continuous experience of ecstasy is your birthright, if you are willing to step up and accept it. There is nothing that can shake or destroy you when you remain conscious. The most challenging part is to feel ecstasy during the seemingly painful events of life. If you can trust that there is truly nothing 'bad' or 'good' about any event or experience, and that "all experiences lead to growth" if seen in the right light, then ultimately there will be an acceptance, an inner balancing, and a diminishing of personal pain. Inner balance invites the experience of ecstasy. When you continuously live in the experience of ecstasy, you constantly attract nurturing events into your life because ecstasy is your template of manifestation. Ecstasy brings more ecstasy. This is a big shift from the old pattern of victimization attracting more victimization. The new inner peace takes hold within and optimism becomes your new template.

Masculine Boundaries

Boundaries are mechanisms, spaces or barriers we use to selectively and protectively control our relationships with other people. The ways in which boundaries operate and the reasons they are designated vary greatly within different relationships. Individuals and entire cultures have different needs for boundaries. Safety and comfort are the major reasons we create these protections. Boundaries serve an entire spectrum of services, from survival (fencing bears out) to emotional contentment (not letting your mother live with you). Accordingly, boundaries can be made of wooden sticks or can be a product of simply speaking your truth. The general purpose of boundaries is to protect a space in which you can grow. The space can exist in physical reality or it can be a space within you.

Boundaries are built and maintained by your positive masculine energy to provide the space for your feminine to be fully alive. If she is protected by masculine boundaries, her feminine nectar can abundantly come forth because she is safe. Healthy boundaries allow more nectar. Delicate flowers bloom best when sheltered from wind and cold temperatures. Protect your feminine and give her a chance to bloom.

When we speak of boundaries, mostly, we are talking about interpersonal boundaries that are maintained in daily relationships with others. Boundaries always come to the foreground when situations arise between people. "Will you watch my dog while I'm away?" "Do you want to have sex right now?" "When are you moving out?" "What did your brother say about me?" "Want to go on vacation together?" "When are we going to have a baby?" "I never want to speak to you again!" "I will not talk to you until next Friday!" Such questions and remarks are challenging. They require thoughtful, feeling responses and major considerations about personal boundaries.

Such situations bring up many different responses from various people. Fear, anger, defensiveness, concern, shame, depression, anxiety, and other emotions may come up when someone challenges your existing boundaries. Your emotional reaction to setting boundaries lets you know what still needs to be healed in your life. It shows you what you are most reactive to, and the process demands that you stand your ground in your positive masculine by setting clear boundaries.

You know you are getting clearer when someone challenges your boundaries and you can very calmly say "no" with a simple explanation. This is 'acting' and not 'reacting,' and is a sign that you are beginning to free yourself. Healthy boundaries come from a place of knowing your own consciousness. Boundaries are logical, simple, ethical, and loving expressions of truth. If the other person can not hear this type of truth, and cannot respect clear boundaries, then it may not be possible to have any future relationship with them. This is a major way to exercise your knowingness. You need to say what is true for you in order to keep your environment supportive.

A boundary is a verbal or written agreement between two people, which hopefully makes life better for both of them. These agreements can perform many functions, from keeping people closer, to keeping them further apart. Once a new boundary is set, everyone can relax more easily. The healthy masculine holds the boundary, so you can relax and create from Source. Everything works better when the balance between masculine and feminine is monitored and boundaries altered with each changing moment.

A boundary can be considered a 'filter' for incoming reality. There are unlimited forms of incoming energy that we must filter for our own good. For instance, we choose to live in certain neighborhoods to control which kind of people live around us. By speaking only one language we are limited to cultures that speak our language. These are basic boundaries that buffer our relationship to the world.

The specific boundaries we choose depend on our previous experiences and the amount of pain that we still hold within.

Do a boundary inventory of your life. Honestly ask yourself how you have defined your boundaries with the key people in your life. Where do you let them cross your line? Do you have a line? What happens if they violate your boundaries regularly? Do you express your feelings directly to them? What happens when you do not figure out that your line has been crossed until the next day? Do you continue to have relationships with people that keep crossing into your safety zone? Do you feel victimized by them? Are you angry? Are you depressed? Boundaries can bring up all of these issues. If you can keep your boundaries in place, you will be expressing your masculine energy in a healthier way.

These observations will help you formulate the improved boundaries that you know you need to establish for the future. These are places where you have not felt comfortable in your relationships. This lack of ease creates nervousness that drives your thoughts into the past and the future to search for answers instead of being present. It is time to resolve the rough spots in your personal relationships so you can move forward more ecstatically. Establishing strong boundaries can assist in this process.

Determine the best way to communicate with each of your friends to establish better boundaries. Decide whether you need to speak with them now or later. Take real action using your positive masculine energy. This practice cleans up your life. Eventually, you will hear your intuition speaking if your boundaries are being challenged by someone else. You will immediately know the answer and have the wisdom to set the perfect boundary in that moment.

If you are not sure of how to set a boundary which will best serve you, take your time. If someone asks you to do something that you are not sure about, tell them you need some time and you will get back to them. If you make a quick, bad decision, call that person back later and say, "After thinking about that, I realize I just can't do it." This is very empowering, and you will feel much more comfortable by being clear with other people. The more you practice with everyone in your life, the easier life gets. People actually stop challenging you when you are clear about your boundaries. Source gets the message that you know what you want, so, what you want is what comes to you. Your inner template begins to consciously manifest in your outer life.

Keep watching all of your choices. Are you choosing what you think you should? Are you choosing what you would enjoy? Are you making choices based on other people's desires? Are you letting others influence your choices? Do you really know what you want? Do you choose certain things under pressure, based on emotions? Boundaries are all about choices and getting your choices recognized and realized in the physical world. Boundaries are about filtering out what you do not want in your life. They help you avoid distractions and keep the feminine space protected.

A healthy boundary is based on positive masculine personal authority which is tempered by a sensitive and loving positive feminine side. The idea is to get what you want while acting graciously. The bottom line is to lovingly say what you want with broadband insight into the present moment. This takes development of the positive feminine power to have patience and understanding in any situation. This is the art of truly mixing hard truth (positive masculine) and compassionate love (positive feminine). Sensitive blending of masculine and feminine brings success. One of the greatest misconceptions is that if you love someone, you do not need boundaries. Love is always a balance of mercy (positive feminine) and severity (positive masculine).

Watch yourself and see how your boundaries are functioning. Are they too loose, too tight or too crazy? Are you getting clearer about what works for you? Do you over-react to others when you just need to say a calm "no"? Use this practice as a way to monitor this important part of your masculine energy. If you are having trouble with boundaries, look at other parts of your negative masculine and make adjustments where they are needed. See if you may need to, literally, get some people out of your life. Keep track of what you need to say to each of the people on your lists and say those things at the appropriate times. Be honest about what you can and can not do and be clear with those who need to know.

In the beginning, it is scary to set boundaries. There is often a fear of loss of friendship or fear of disapproval. The truth is, setting honest boundaries is usually a catalyst to positive change in your life. Those people who become angry about your commitment to meeting your own needs should not be in your life. Your real supporters will be happy that you are getting clearer on what you want and they will support you. It is time to get honest, get clear, and get what you really want from life. Appropriate boundary-setting by the positive masculine is the key. Don't be afraid to say what works and what doesn't work for you. Don't let other people waste your time. Be firm, loving, and clear with everyone in your life by setting boundaries that bring more Grace into your life. Raise your own bar and create a higher quality of life by taking actions that demonstrate you respect yourself.

SEEING WITHIN YOUR LOVER

Your relationship with your lover is a mirror image, a direct out-picturing of the state of balance between your inner feminine and your inner masculine. Therefore, your relationship offers you the perfect opportunity on a daily basis to watch as your inner template fluctuates moment to moment in your lover's presence. In this way, your love relationship can teach you much of what you still need to learn about yourself. The changing balance of your own unique inner template specifically attracts and continues to desire reciprocal engagement with your lover. Your perfections and distortions are standing right in front of you, in the form of your lover's actions or reactions to your own behavior. This constant feedback can show you where you still need to look within yourself.

This process of seeing within your lover is as direct as you can get to seeing with clarity your inner balance, because all the buttons being pushed are your own. That is why blaming your lover is a waste of time and unproductive for you both. You actually only have yourself to look at, as your lover is mirroring your imbalances back to you. If you can consciously utilize this type of analysis, you will mature very quickly. To take total responsibility requires incredible humility, and at the same time you must avoid being victimized by the process. Remember each interaction with your lover is a mirror of yourself. This is not an easy process, as it is likely you will be habitually drawn to your old way, which is to blame others for whatever is not feeling comfortable to you.

Humility is the key. You have to be willing to realize that whatever your lover presents to you is really 'a look in the mirror.' That is challenging for many people. To make use of this form of self-analysis, you need to be honest with yourself. Also, you must accept that you have drawn your lover to you, and that your lover is the perfect gift to currently assist in your own evolution. This fits into the esoteric understanding that "everything is a gift yet unwrapped." Our process of maturing brings us both painful gifts and pleasant gifts. It is helpful not to judge our painful experiences as 'negative.' If you can take responsibility for all the experiences you draw to yourself, including your lover's responses to you, then you are able to be more honest with yourself.

Let's say you are one of those rare people who can actually take responsibility for seeing all of the manifestations in your life as resulting from your inner template. Therefore, you have already accepted that your lover is somehow a manifestation of your inner self. The manifestation is not always the same as what is within you. It may be opposite or sideways of where you are. However, the mirroring is exactly what you need to see in that moment about yourself. Your most significant unresolved issues create physical, emotional and mental events between you, your partner, and with the world in general. Remember, you may have to look deeply, because there is not always an obvious direct relationship between the part you see in your lover and the part that needs healing within you. Always consider the opposites.

If you continue to apply this principle of self-awareness, there will come a time where you do not react to your partner's issues. At that point, your conscious analysis of the mirroring process will be successful. If your partner's 'bad habits' continue after you have consistently stayed neutral around them, it may be time to take a deeper look at your future with that person. You can outgrow other people and it happens frequently. Partners may come and go as your inner balance unfolds in your world. You will always be improving the quality of your future life by working on your inner balance. As your self-integrity matures, you can also expect to experience more balance in the physical manifestations of your life.

The inner balance between your feminine and masculine aspects improves as you consciously work with your relationships. Your growing awareness will show you that what serves your evolution today is much different than what worked for you even a few years ago. It is helpful to acknowledge that each experience, every moment, is a wonderful opportunity to become more conscious and to more fully integrate Source-consciousness until self becomes Self. At the point of Self-realization, it is impossible to blame anyone for anything. As a co-creator with Source, you are fully responsible for your own life. Personal freedom comes from this realization. You are empowered as you let go of the idea of victimization. There is no longer any place for blame.

Working with your lover to see within yourself is best done directly with your lover, so that you can fully interact to experience the deepest mirroring possible. In most of your other relationships it is usually advised that you work out the issues that come up for you with people away from them in your own personal space. For the love relationship to serve both partners, it demands regular interaction and discussion about what is happening at every level. This can be a very challenging process to do with your lover and requires humility, sensitivity and especially willingness from both of you. If both partners are not equally willing to use the relationship in this way, this is not advised. It is best to wait until your hearts are truly open to each other before beginning.

Becoming sensitive is mostly about listening without the usual instant reactions to old story lines which so quickly possess the mind. You will want to stay conscious by listening from your heart and by listening to your emotional self. If you only hear in the old mental way, then the tendency is to talk about 'old wound story,' which is really old pain inside of you being activated by your lover in the present moment. You have a choice. You can either blame your partner, which is the old way of reacting, or you can use the experience as an opportunity to go more deeply into your own pain, the wound that was probably there before you ever met your lover.

In such a circumstance with your lover, you have to determine if you would be best served to process the wound right in that moment in front of your partner or whether you need to take a look at it later by yourself where you may feel safer. A future safe place might be at your therapist's office, in your bedroom by yourself, or with a friend. Let's say you feel safe enough with your lover to process your pain right in that moment. Then, you both make a conscious agreement to stay present and the process begins.

Below is a detailed example of a mirroring process between two lovers. You can apply these same principles with your lover:

Your lover has just told you that she cannot be with you for the holidays because she needs to visit her mother at that time. Your first reaction could be to get angry and blame her for not being there during your vacation from work. You might get outraged and scream, "I'm so mad!...I finally have some time off and you run off to hang out with your friends back home...You could care less about me...You are so selfish...I hate you!..."

It is important to look honestly at both versions of reality here. Your lover is concerned about her mom. She is feeling a lot of guilt about being away from her mom since dad died just three months ago. She does not want mom to be alone on her first Christmas without dad. Who will take care of mom? Your partner feels compelled to do the right thing. She probably hasn't even had time to think about your needs.

You think that your feelings have not been honored and how dare your lover take off when you need her. This feeling in you, which you are blaming on your partner, is your indicator that something has to change. Rather than thinking about why she's leaving and does she love you and how could she be so inconsiderate, you have to go inside yourself at this very moment and ask, "Which of my wounds has been activated here?" "Why am I so uncomfortable with this situation?" "When did something like this happen before in my life that brought up these same feelings?" "Do these same feelings come in other situations with other people?" "When was the first time I felt like this?" "How do I really feel at the deepest level in this moment?"

In this example, the deepest level of pain has nothing to do with the initial anger. A deeper look reveals that the feelings you are experiencing are associated with the fact that you were abandoned by your mother at an early age. The planned departure of your lover is a huge trigger for the grief you hold subconsciously around not getting the love you craved as a child. Of course, this particular example is hypothetical, but similar scenarios are actually very common for many people. The point is to use the trigger to go inside and to stop blaming others for your feelings. They are *your* feelings and you have to accept them by taking responsibility to live with them or to heal them.

Continuing with this example, let's say you are able to look within and to realize the deeper abandonment wound originates in your early child relationship with your mother. Now you can deal with this situation in a much more conscious way. You can turn to your partner and try a new approach. You might say, "When you told me you were leaving for Christmas to visit your mom, my first reaction was to feel very angry with you." This is honest and is not acting out your anger. You are simply telling her your emotional truth.

Then, you could say something like, "After reflecting on this situation, I realize that beneath this anger, I am actually feeling a lot of grief…I also know that this means I have not completely dealt with the pain I felt when I was young around my issues of abandonment." Then, you could even say, "I know how much pressure you must feel about watching over your mom since your dad died so recently, and your mom is all alone." This type of approach encourages intimacy, and you are still not compromising your truth. There is a good chance that now she can even support you, since she better understands why you feel the way you do. If you both feel safe enough, the process could be completed by her holding you while you cry. This example demonstrates how balancing of the inner masculine and feminine can increase your awareness of yourself and your lover and positively affect your life. Apply this type of analysis to your love relationship and see yourself in the mirror of love.

Seeing Within External Relationships

You can expand your view of your own inner balance by looking at certain relationships with other significant people in your life. All interpersonal relationships reflect some aspect of the nature of your own inner balance. Take a look at the different varieties of relationships that exist. The different categories of relationship include parent-child, brother-sister, friends, employer-employee, doctor-patient, co-workers, as well as lovers. These relationships all can teach you about yourself. Potentially, the insights you gain are a vehicle for personal growth.

This process involves seeing how you interact within several significant relationships in your life. Think of several other important people in your life with whom you may have challenges. Ask yourself, "Who are the most difficult people in my life at this time?" Look among your family members, friends, employer, neighbors, and co-workers to find the relationships you are ready to study. There are usually about ten or less of these people in your life. The people that you continually talk about and think about are the ones that you should work with here.

Later, we will do a formal Practical Exercise to work with this material, but for now, begin to scan your relationships and watch how you affect others and how they affect you. See your challenges, the rough spots in your relationship with each of them. These 'dislikes' are the issues that cause you to become emotionally reactive when dealing with them. Identify relationships where certain stimuli cause predictable emotional reactions. These repeating patterns show us the most about our deepest imbalances.

Also consider the things you like the most about these people, what you enjoy about them and why you are grateful to be in relationship with each of them. By focusing on their positive aspects, you will begin to see them in a more positive way. Whatever you focus on gets bigger.

Let insights come to you intuitively. You can also start to notice whether you think in terms of 'likes' or 'dislikes.' This allows you to see how positive you are, or are not. By using this new way of seeing all of the time, your experience of life will change. Your perception will expand into a broader bandwidth and you will see more deeply into yourself and others.

Focus on these people on an ongoing daily basis. Watch every situation as you interact with each of them. Watch them in person, by phone, on e-mails, on text messages, and note any intuitive insights you have. Look at the obvious things like their facial expressions, verbal responses, and emotional responses. Notice how you are feeling each time you are around them, or interacting with them. What are they mirroring to you in every moment you spend with them? The best insights often come when you are away from that person and being quiet with yourself.

To use this process successfully, you must become the non-biased Observer of the person you are seeing and of yourself at the same time. This takes real focus and patience. You are literally watching everything that is being projected by their words, body language, tone of voice, timing of conversation, energy level, emotional response, and even their level of interest in being with you. Watch all of these clues and really see yourself in the mirror.

At the same time, you must be aware of you. How did you feel before you approached them? How do you feel about this connection? Is old history with them running through your mind as you are communicating in the present? How much of your current reaction is due to unsettled stuff from the past? Are you even listening to them or just trying to make your point? Is this conversation going anywhere? These are just a few things to be aware of while you are with anyone.

Focusing on these questions and being honest about the answers is extremely helpful in gaining insight into yourself. Such focus will bring a new level of awareness into your relationships as you learn to observe the other while remaining aware of your own actions at the same time. We are always acting as mirrors for each other. Accepting this truth helps us take responsibility for how we bring actions and emotions upon ourselves based on how we treat others. Once you take an honest look at your relationships using this 'mirror-like wisdom,' you actually can enjoy a more pleasant life. Positive change occurs because you give up a sense of victimization and step into the role of co-creator with Source. Once you can see that people are mirroring your own patterns back to you, you will no longer blame them for their actions. Instead, you will begin to take even greater responsibility for your own actions.

You create your own reality. Other people help you see yourself more clearly. Other people often mirror by opposite action. For example, maybe you are too frugal and they are too extravagant. People also mirror you directly. Maybe you are feeling guilty about spending too much money and your friend says, "My spending is way out of control." So whether it comes directly or by opposite example, you must be humble enough to take responsibility for your own judged weaknesses or failings as mirrored to you through other people. Sometimes something as simple as overhearing a conversation at the grocery store check-out line directly speaks to your life. In this case, words from a stranger, a minor player in your reality, can be the key to changing your entire life.

Listen with an open mind and open heart. Remember that the other person is there at the perfect time to give you an important message that you need to hear in that moment. Source perfectly serves you at any time you are willing to consciously participate. Experiences with other people can be painful. If you focus on the bigger message and not on the pain, you will grow faster. If you try to avoid the naturally painful experiences of life, you actually prolong the suffering. What you avoid will come back more emphatically the next time until you finally humble yourself enough to truly listen. This doesn't mean that you should force yourself to stay in difficult personal relationships for long periods. Ultimately, if the real message is to leave a bad situation, the challenge is to do it with grace.

As you no longer blame others in difficult situations, you can not blame yourself. There can be no regrets. All experiences are for self-growth. However, you now have the information to make better choices next time. This is the purpose of all your life scenarios. Make better choices based on your recent experiences. This focuses your life in real, present time, holding your focus in the moment. This keeps your relationships current and honest without old baggage or future apprehensions. Being fully aware in the present is essential to this work.

As you do this practice, can you stay current in real time? It takes a lot of trust to stay in the moment. The key is to align your personal will with Source in such a way that you can personally receive guidance from Source constantly and follow what you hear. This process requires a certain amount of stillness in your mind. Stillness is the correct environment for the non-reactive Observer and the conscious Actor. The beginning of this practice is to be still and listen to Source. Once you trust that connection, you can begin to act in the world from Source intelligence. Living in this way allows you to remain fully conscious in each moment and allows you to be fully responsible for each of your actions. This is an ongoing practice which requires years to develop fully. Be patient with yourself.

The Inner Balance

The lovers are symbolized by a man looking at a woman and the woman is looking up to Source. This is really a metaphor for how our consciousness should work. Self-consciousness (masculine) looks to sub-consciousness (feminine) who then looks to supra-consciousness (Source). Every part of this triad is equally valuable and each is needed for proper functioning of the whole. By more fully understanding how each part participates, you can consciously work with this triad of consciousness to become more aware. See how each of these parts works within you and start to make changes that bring more unified manifestation from your Self.

If any of the three – masculine self-consciousness, feminine sub-consciousness, and Source supra-consciousness - are not considered, balance is lost. Therefore, no part of the triad is more important than another. You need to be constantly aware of each component and always be pliable enough to instantaneously shift the focus from one part of the triad to another. This requires constant introspection by your Observer Self. By being this aware, you can monitor yourself moment by moment and live more consciously in the flow of life as it unfolds around you. This is the practice of being here now and fully participating.

Let's follow the healthy process of manifestation from its beginning at Source. All possibilities are present at that initial level. It is a big Universe with many dimensions and many other types of manifestation besides what we know here on Earth. Ultimate reality has a very large bandwidth. Humans perceive and interact with only a very small spectrum of the broadband of reality. We can consciously intend to broaden our personal bandwidth by balancing our masculine and feminine.

The easiest analogy would be to look at the ability of humans to perceive light. We only see light frequencies that lie in the visible spectrum between ultraviolet (higher frequency) and infrared (lower frequency). Therefore, this is the only reality that we can directly perceive without tools. But this is not the only reality that exists. Somehow, we find ways to see the unseen and manifest the unseen into physical reality. Using this analogy, humans have built machines that can 'see' infrared and ultraviolet light. But, how did we know that there were unseen light frequencies in the first place? Here is where feminine intuition comes in.

The mind is a closed box much like a computer. There are a limited number of bits of data that can be re-patterned into different configurations. Manifestation is limited by the specific data that is available within the closed system. The possible spectrum of manifestation is limited unless we bring in new bits of data to combine with existing information. This process of bringing in new data from the unseen is the role of the feminine. Visions, dreams, and intuitions are ways we see the unseen.

Science (masculine) is a closed system. The most respected scientists are the ones that have the longest resumes. They are entrenched in the old story because they must quote references to old science and must slowly advance their new concepts, while holding on to the core of the old beliefs which may simply be false. This is the scientific method that binds us to the past and does not encourage us to see the unseen.

The most brilliant scientists are ones who break the paradigm. The greatest scientists like Albert Einstein or Nicola Tesla had visions about the unseen laws of nature that broke from the old beliefs. These quantum leaps in knowledge allow the mind to generate new formulas because there is new insight to circulate with old data. Feminine connection with Source is the first step in this process of healthy manifestation. These two scientists were in touch with their feminine side enough to be able to see beyond the limitations of their masculine minds.

The first step in manifestation is the vision. A person has a vision of a possible reality. No one else may even know that this has happened unless the positive masculine energy is engaged. The vision is seen but without the masculine as the bridge, manifestation does not occur yet. The process usually begins with mental dialog within self. The mind begins to turn around with the new data. Many new possibilities arise and must be evaluated in reference to the old paradigm. How does it fit? What could it mean? Where do we go from here? Do I really need to let go of that false old idea? Now we have entered the realm of masculine mind.

Usually, after the first vision, there will be more bursts of intuition. Often it takes multiple inspirations to see the bigger picture implicit in the initial vision. At this point there is a possibility that the process can be thwarted by the negative masculine ego. For example, the first vision comes through the positive feminine and the negative masculine grabs the vision and says, "I've got it and now I know the answer." This arrogance (negative masculine) then interrupts the flow from the positive feminine and only one small piece of the puzzle is revealed. On the other hand, if the person is balanced enough in their masculine and feminine, the soul remains open to Source, no matter what. This open positive feminine is essential for seeing the whole picture in every aspect of life.

What is unseen plays an integral role in creating our reality whether we understand it or not. If we do not remain aware of how this process works, then it is easy to feel victimized (negative feminine) by life. If we understand how our thoughts manifest from dreams and intuitions into the physical, then we are taking our place as co-creators with Source. We are no longer victims. It has been said that magic is no longer magic when we know the rules of Source and apply those laws consciously. Disconnection from Source through lack of acknowledgment of the unseen (feminine subconscious) is ignorance (negative masculine). By exploring the inner world of dreams and meditation (both positive feminine) we can learn about the normally unseen laws of the Universe and begin to apply them consciously. This is true power and it requires positive feminine energy.

Here is an example of how this works. Let's say that your antenna is up and your positive feminine is receiving truthful, intuitive input. Now, what do you do with that intuitive information? Your positive masculine needs to step up and take charge to form the bridge to manifestation while still remaining in the flow of feminine intuition. This is a critical moment of balance, because the masculine alone will mess it up. It is the blending of intuition and mental knowledge that creates perfected manifestation. If all goes well, any action toward the goal of making the 'unseen seen' is monitored and continually modified by intuition. The monitoring often comes via the emotions. Does this feel right? Am I enjoying the process or just doing what I think I have to do? When the mental and emotional aspects of your being are both encouraging you to take action, then it is probably safe to do so. We need to wait for this internal 'green light' before moving ahead in life.

This is an introspective process. Watching all levels of consciousness at the same time and being open to our intuition allows us to make choices that will be good for all aspects of our self. If we act prematurely, as soon as we think we 'know,' we really have cut ourselves off from true knowing. The situation at hand is often bigger than what our little minds know. We are limited by our receptive bandwidth. That is why we must always be open to the intuitive feminine, seeing within the unseen, and looking beyond what we think we know. This requires patience and great humility. This is what the negative masculine forgets. As soon as the negative masculine cuts himself off from his positive feminine, he cuts himself off from Source and his manifestation will be controlled by his basic ego urges.

The negative patriarchy has controlled this planet politically, socially, and especially economically for thousands of years. Decisions have been made by a small group of negative-masculine-minded men, which have affected everyone on the planet. These men have one agenda – power, through controlling the money of the masses for their own personal gain. There is no intuition involved in their agenda. They have 'closed-box minds' that continually re-state old agendas. They are cut off from their positive feminine nature with no regard for the unseen nature of true reality. They are not living in the moment or responding to the deeper implications of current situations. They are blind to the bigger picture.

The problem with patriarchal leadership on Earth is that many societies are patterned by these negative masculine principles. Children are not taught about inner balance. No one is taught to honor the feminine. In Western society, the value of meditation is only beginning to be acknowledged in recent years. Western children are taught that poor people and poor cultures are worthless. Lies regarding the true nature of reality are widespread. Yet, the truth can still be found within each of us.

If the leaders on Earth are not teaching children to listen to Source and to value it, then how will this ever change? The old ways are so ingrained in us that it's going to take a major situation to change global priorities. For now, it takes individuals who must step up one at a time and do things differently without society's support. It requires real strength to reclaim the Truth and to live in balance with Source. Honoring intuition has been the missing essential ingredient in society for a long time. We have been manifesting from the negative masculine ego for centuries. But now we have the tools to become more integrated. As we do this individually, we allow that new integration to step into the world of form.

Let's say you are functioning more effectively because your intuition and mind are more integrated, and you have an inspiration. Your visions (positive feminine) still need to be manifested into physical reality using the positive masculine steps previously outlined (see Masculine Energy chapter). A plan is made, the goal is set, and action begins. Focus must remain on the entire situation. A steadfast daily commitment must be adhered to continuously. Your emotions must be acknowledged but must not stop the process of action, unless that is the specific message from the positive feminine. The negative feminine can get in the way here. If the doer is obsessed by emotional pain (negative feminine), the pain can actually stop the correct course of action (negative masculine). Therefore, if emotions control your mind, you will be ineffective. Yet, if you completely ignore your emotions, you will also be ineffective since you will not be open to Source.

As I explained before, emotions are associated with the element of water. Tears of joy or pain are literally the water moving out of your body. Though a miraculous substance, water's intrinsic nature is its instability. Water can take the form of ice, water or steam. Depending on the environment, water changes form very quickly due to changing temperatures. This analogy carries through for emotions. Emotions do the same thing. If you are in an inspiring, organically-balanced environment, it is easier to remain calm and joyful. If you are in a war zone, it is common to be terrorized or grief-stricken. If you are fighting with your spouse, rage can come. Emotions change very rapidly and unpredictably.

Emotions make very poor masters of your life because of their unpredictability. Emotions can take you off your center and spin you around until you have forgotten your purpose or direction. This is the essence of the negative feminine. When this spinning occurs, you must find a still point (positive feminine) and regain your grounding (positive masculine) in order to accomplish anything. This is when you need to call the positive masculine forth and find your footing again.

The quality and beauty of your manifestations are dependent upon your ability to balance your personal masculine and feminine in every moment. By accomplishing this, you are always in the flow of co-creating with Source and you always know how to take that flow into the next moment. There is also more likelihood of avoiding future problems because your actions have more integrity. Source will not guide you into dis-ease or dis-harmony when you remain open to the ongoing messages. The flow is always present and the challenge is how fully you can participate with it in your life. The inner balance of your masculine and your feminine is your core of sanity and the template for future healthy manifestation.

Inner Dialogue

Learn to know the different voices of your masculine and feminine aspects. Once you identify which part is speaking, you can learn more about your personal state of internal balance. Which half is the predominant force within you? How do the masculine and feminine treat each other, especially under pressure? How conscious are you of your inner template? What are your inner masculine and feminine teaching you about Self? How can you consciously intervene in the externalization of your inner template? Watch, listen, and learn about yourself. See how to work with your masculine and feminine energies to maximize positive manifestations. Keep your Observer Self ever-vigilant.

Who runs your show most of the time? Is it your masculine energy or does the feminine usually take the lead? This makes a huge difference in how you present yourself to the world, beginning with the active and passive polarity which directly relates to introversion and extroversion. Masculine-dominant people (men or women) tend to be more active, more extroverted, and more 'go getters.' Feminine-dominant people tend to be more passive, introverted, and reflective by nature. These are very broad statements which speak to the most general nature of masculine and feminine energies.

Let's use an example from this broader prospective. Let's say that George is operating predominantly from his feminine. He keeps to himself and doesn't get out much. He is an artist with a studio at home. He's married to Joan who is masculine-dominant and who loves to work at the bank as the manager. She has no interest in having children because she has never had much maternal instinct. George has difficulty selling his work and gets depressed frequently. Joan tries to encourage him to socialize and go to counseling, but he does neither. He gets angry at Joan much of the time. She's always working and doing things around town, and when she finally does stop, her mind continues to run constantly. Neither George nor Joan sleep very well and their sex life is non-existent. They are gaining weight.

In this example, the externalized relationship becomes the balance for both George and Joan because neither of them has found balance within themselves. They are both using each other to get what they have not recognized and have not been able to provide for themselves individually. This sets up dependency upon each other and encourages abdication of personal responsibility. George needs Joan's money (masculine) and Joan needs George to get in touch with her own emotional self (feminine). George needs someone to think for him (masculine) so he can survive another week at the house. Joan needs to slow down and check in with herself and feel her way (feminine) into her future.

As long as we depend on others to 'feel our feelings' and take care of our personal responsibilities, we continue to be victims of life. We continue to get angry and to blame others for what we refuse to look at and deal with each day. Looking truthfully at self is one of the most effective ways to assure evolution of consciousness. If not now, when? How many more people are you going to blame before you take responsibility for your own life? How much pain are you willing to live with before you make the hard choice to do something to change?

In describing the differences between masculine and feminine, the general qualities are active/passive, mental/emotional, and doing/being. These terms are helpful but they can only take us so far because the differentiation is not that black and white. As an example, if we were to listen carefully to what we could call the 'active' versus the 'passive' attributes of sound, we would hear an entire spectrum of possibilities. On the active end we would have clanging, banging, exploding, sirens, ringing, and popping. On the passive end of the spectrum we would have whispering, tapping, whisking, twitching, and slithering sounds. Not only are there differences in tonal quality, but also we experience volume and clarity differences.

This same spectrum of variation is true of masculine and feminine energies. There is a basic difference and that difference plays out in many unique ways. Begin to pay attention to the subtle energies and the 'tone' of what is around you. You are an intuitive person, and you have a great capacity to be even more intuitive, if you pay more attention. You can be more finely tuned into the emotions that surround you by first focusing on your own feelings. How do I feel? Where do I feel it in my body? What happened just before I started to feel this? How does it feel to allow myself to feel? How are other people feeling to me when they are around me? Are those feelings related to me? Am I taking other people's emotions too personally? Am I over-indulging my emotions? Am I honest with others about my feelings? This kind of self-observation allows your feminine to give you valid input.

To include your masculine, be aware of what you are thinking, doing, and planning in any particular situation. Masculine self-observation would include such questions as: What do you think about your progress, so far? Why are you doing what you're doing? When will it be complete? How are you going to resolve a particular problem? When you are in touch with your masculine, the analysis and action continues. See within the patterns. See how your consciousness automatically goes in certain directions at certain times. Learn your patterns so you can resolve to change negative ones. Choose to get off automatic pilot and start to live consciously in every moment.

It is worthwhile to ask yourself the big question, "How did I get here?" How did I become the person I am today? What was the sequence of events that formed my life and shaped me into the person I am now? It is useful to identify cause and effect. It is even more valuable to trace the emotional path between causes and effects. Unresolved pain is usually what keeps you caught up in these loops of cause and effect. The way you act or react to others is a result of your stored emotions and belief systems.

Becoming fully conscious of your emotional patterns is an effective way to change your actions. You need to spot the old patterns as they arise in each moment in order to make different choices to act with others in new ways. Counseling is a great way to gain insights into your inner template, as we often need outside input to see ourselves. If counseling is not possible or not your choice, then at least utilize your own Observer Self to see yourself more clearly. Listen to Source and choose your actions carefully with as much consciousness as possible. Self-awareness is the path to freedom, and everything you need is within your own consciousness, if you can learn to listen.

Keep working on releasing your emotional baggage until you do not hear any more static in your head. The static is the argument within you that starts with old emotional pain, the old story being played out in response to situations which are currently triggering you. The work of balancing masculine and feminine within yourself means working with all the pain which causes you to act out from these old stories. Once the pain is felt and traced back to its cause, it will resolve, and you can better hear Source and live accordingly, without static. When you are able to make choices guided directly by Source, without static, then you are really hearing your intuition. Pain rules your life until this is accomplished. Ignorance is not bliss, it is a life constructed by your unconscious template of pain. You make the choice. Once the baggage is cleared and you are healthier, you can 'act' instead of 'react' to life around you.

BEING WHILE DOING

Everyone – man or woman - has both masculine and feminine energies that are expressed independently and uniquely. Pure states of masculine or feminine energy are not effective for very long without the balancing effect of the opposite aspect. For example, if you are only operating out of your feminine energy, you will not have any boundaries with other people because boundaries are a masculine function. The converse example is, if you live only in your masculine, you will not be able to access intuition from Source and you will be limited by the constraints of your mind. Effectiveness is dependent upon blending your masculine and feminine aspects together consciously and appropriately. The changing ratio of your inner balance is ideally determined by what is happening each moment around you.

This blending process is the art of inner balance. The intention of this book is to assist you in learning how to observe yourself while simultaneously altering your actions to live in balance each moment in the world. Primarily and most importantly, this is about being more conscious of yourself. As this is mastered, the next task is to simultaneously watch how those around you are mirroring parts of yourself to you. Life is truly a multi-dimensional experience. You are the neutral Observer and the conscious Actor, simultaneously. Your consciousness has the capability to be in at least two places at one time. Seeing within actually stimulates brain function in new multi-tasking modes which teach the brain to work holographically. This allows the brain to function from several regions at a time, expanding brain function beyond what is normally expected. Usually, we use primarily one cerebral region at one time.

Let's put the inner balancing process into very practical terms. We have just identified the Actor and the Observer within ourselves.

The next step is to rename these parts Doing and Being. Now, we can see how they fluctuate, how they relate to each other in response to environmental situations and other people. When are you the Actor, Doing? When are you the Observer, Being? When are you both at the same time? This ratio is the external expression of your inner balance. We watch to see how we express our personal balance of both parts in the external world. This is important to note, because if we are not expressing healthy balance outwardly, then there is no internal balance either.

There are often so many layers of emotional pain that people do not look deeply enough to find their core emotional patterns. The analysis of personal inner balance is a method of seeing more deeply into what is really driving superficial emotional states. Your initial emotional response is usually not a true reflection of the deeper wounds which are driving it. It is your responsibility to always look as deeply as possible into your yet unrevealed self to find the early sources of pain. Attending to these wounds is a way to speed the healing process.

For example, Lydia goes to her therapist and says that she is depressed. She has withdrawn from her husband emotionally and sexually for over a year. The therapist asks many questions and finally Lydia admits that she is enraged with her husband. She is to the point of exasperation and will not even speak to him anymore. She is repulsed by many of his common mannerisms. Using inner balance analysis, the therapist helps the woman understand herself better.

The therapist delves a little deeper and asks Lydia if screaming at him has ever helped her relationship with her husband. She says, "No. He withdraws and leaves me alone. He won't even talk to me. This behavior goes on for hours, on and on, until it hurts really badly." The therapist says, "I understand that you are in a lot of pain.

How long have you been in pain? Were you in pain any time before your marriage with your husband?" Lydia says, "Since my dad died, when I was twelve. It's been hard to trust men. Men have betrayed me time and time again. I still do not trust men. I'm so angry! I wish I could hurt them all!" The therapist responds, "I'll bet it's hard to trust your husband." Lydia starts to cry. She finally connects the dots. She sees beyond the superficial layer of anger into the underlying unconscious fear of abandonment and betrayal which has been directing her life for so long.

She has held this fear in her sub-conscious since she was twelve years old. Fear of further abandonment has controlled her adult life and has caused her to act out in many unhealthy ways. Unacknowledged fear has caused her to unconsciously act out anger in an attempt to control her husband. Since expressing her anger did not bring her peace, she became depressed. She has also used this same strategy to deal with many other people in her life.

In a similar way, you can explore your own emotional layers using the specifics of your life, or the lives of those people you know. See if you can define the layers of emotion that define each person's life strategy, from the most superficial layer to the deepest one. Once you see these patterns consciously, you can make swift changes in your life through your new self-awareness.

Now that Lydia is conscious of the fact that her anger (negative masculine) toward her husband starts with her fear (negative feminine), she can work on her fear and abandonment issues in therapy. These realizations allow her to stop acting out her anger (negative masculine) on her husband. This allows him to relax (positive feminine) and to be more present (positive feminine) with her because he is no longer the object of her anger (negative masculine). Now he feels safer to reach out and nurture her. Healing comes through deeper inner awareness.

It is interesting to note that in our example, Lydia's husband would always go away (negative feminine) when she became angry (negative masculine). This plugged right into the abandonment fear (negative feminine) that she had had since her father's death. The wisdom of Source always promotes deeper healing and inner balance. Scenarios and circumstances that keep pushing your buttons will continue to arise until you finally get the deeper messages. The external challenges usually become more and more intense until you finally 'get it.' Life is much easier when you stay conscious, watching yourself and altering your actions in every situation to lead to greater ease and more Grace. Self awareness allows you to make your own changes before painful experiences force you to make them.

Practice the art of Doing while Being until you do not even have to think about it as a process anymore. It becomes a normal part of your daily conscious awareness. This takes time, honesty, humility, sensitivity, love, compassion, and patience. It takes constant attention and the courage to confront your deepest pain and to allow yourself to feel it. You need strength to stay with your pain, sometimes for weeks or even months, until you finally reach your deepest wound and are able to release it. This takes perseverance and the willingness to explore new ways to move the pain out of your body, usually using sound and motion release processes.

Study the space between the extremes of your feelings and your behavior. This is the dancing ground of Doing and Being. There is a constant juggling act taking place. See the sphere of Being and the sphere of Doing as two separate but intimately connected mechanisms in your life. Imagine two balls passing each other while being controlled by the one Observer, perfectly giving and taking, with small changes in course based on prevailing breezes. Know yourself as the one Observer who juggles, spins, and plays with them every day, every moment. In consciously taking on this practice, you will see more deeply within your self until eventually there is far less pain to process and far more Grace to enjoy.

Here is another example of a lack of inner balance. Let's say Joe is really hard on himself. He makes unconscious negative statements such as, "I am so fat and ugly. I'm so stupid. I don't have a clue. Nobody likes me. I'm sick all the time." Joe truly expects bad things to happen and they do. This is the Law of Attraction in operation. "Whatever you focus on gets bigger." If Joe focuses on problems he will have more problems. If he focuses on joyful changes in his life, he will manifest that joy. If Joe thinks of himself as intelligent, then others will see his brilliance. Inner balance analysis leads to personal changes that are realized through self-awareness followed by making real life changes that promote more Grace.

Your inner template of emotion (feminine), thought (masculine), and intuition (feminine) truly create your action (masculine). With Self awareness, you can keep it all in balance. Alignment to Source, using both its masculine and feminine aspects, is the key to conscious manifestation. In other words, inner balance literally manifests balanced external relationships. When there is perfect alignment between Source and manifestation, Grace is manifest.

The saying, "Nothing can shake or destroy me," is absolutely true when you remain in a state of balance. By being totally conscious of Self and your surrounding environment, you will always have the perfect knowing to make the perfect response. Once you understand this and integrate this knowledge in your deepest core, you will experience that there is truly nothing to fear. You will no longer go into thoughts of past or future, trusting your old thinking to keep you 'safe.' To live in this state, you need to stay present and listen to Source (positive feminine) and take action (positive masculine) whenever you are instructed to do so. It can be a great challenge to operate this way, particularly when you are under pressure, yet it is the only way to guarantee the best outcome in every situation of your life.

Self-awareness helps to develop self-trust. You will trust yourself more because you will actually know yourself better. Self-trust brings more self-confidence and empowerment. Personal power comes from being willing to feel personal pain and to take personal responsibility for all painful situations that you encounter in your life, without regrets. Exploring your inner template reveals to you how your unconscious fears have created past situations. By consciously revealing and releasing your deepest emotional wounds, you can change your entire life based on developing the core practice of self-awareness. You can also become more self-aware by using your awareness to more completely see other people's patterns and how they are a reflection of your own.

Here is another example of inner balance analysis. Liz is in touch with her feminine. She is full of joy and sensitivity, and she connects well with her intuition on a continual basis. She is an extremely internal, private person who doesn't leave her house very often. At social gatherings, she is usually shy and many people in town do not even know she exists. She still lives with her birth family at age thirty since she does not know how to financially support herself. She spends much of her time writing a book based on her strong intuition. She has no idea how to get the book published.

Liz is the classic archetype of a strong positive inner feminine and a negative inner masculine. It is also interesting to note that her externalized feminine is also negative. She has connection with Source but has no mechanism (positive masculine) to bring her truth (positive feminine) into manifestation. Therefore, she sits quietly with her family imprisoned by her ongoing failure to take any action (negative masculine). In this case, the inner feminine is active but still not really healthy without the blending in of the healthy masculine. She needs both. Liz's is an example which shows that pure feminine on its own fails every time.

The same is true of the pure masculine. Let's say Beth is totally focused on her masculine energy and its development. She regularly goes to the gym. She doesn't get involved in drama with anyone. She's the first one to stand in your face and tell you what a screw-up you are when she gets angry. She never cries. She's insensitive to other people's feelings. She never listens to what other people say. She always knows "how it is." Just ask her. Beth is harsh and unpleasant with most people.

Beth is productive and quite clever about doing things. The problem is that she is not acting intuitively from Source. Beth needs her healthy feminine to hear Source. She needs this information so she can create a more balanced life. Her masculine needs guidance that only her feminine can provide. First being aware of, and then working with her imbalances, could lead her to making new choices that could bring new outcomes into her life.

You can use these examples to see parallels in your own life. See how you, or people in your life, operate in similar ways to Lydia, Joe, Liz, or Beth. Especially, look at the issue of 'layering of emotions.' Try to determine which layer is the primary cause. This is the emotional state that is triggering other emotions to come out secondarily. First addressing the primary emotional layer brings positive changes faster than working with the more superficial repetitive emotional states. Self-awareness and Source guidance combine to provide answers that yield healthy responses in every moment. This is the simultaneous function of Being and Doing that allows Grace to come forth.

GRACE

Grace is the perfect ever-changing balance of movement between your masculine and feminine energies, the divine dance of total awareness of Self with your surrounding environment. When in a state of Grace, you are beautifully co-creating with Source from your inner template (inner balance) which is the foundation of your life. Ideally, you are so aware of your world that you are subtly and continuously modifying your reactions until they transmute into conscious actions. Grace is the experience of living a conscious life in which you are co-creator with Source.

It feels peaceful and joyful to live in Grace. Calmness allows you to be more present in each moment. We have talked about being in the present and why this is so important for receiving insight from your intuition. However, the actual process of being present (positive feminine) can be very challenging. It requires a great amount of will power (positive masculine) to stay focused on the situation directly in front of you. Old habits make it easy to compare the present situation to past events, causing old feelings of regret. Equally, anticipation of some future fear often keeps the mind working overtime to plan strategies for possible problems that might be arising in the future. The challenge is to stop yourself from focusing on past regrets or future fears which keep you from being present wherever you are. Being in present time is the basis of the awareness that you need to do the Practical Exercises described in the next chapter.

You can learn to stop yourself as soon as your Observer sees you moving out of balance. Stop yourself when your Observer sees you breaking one of your own agreements. The challenge is to stop your own patterns as soon as you become conscious of them. When you get good at this, you will be able to stop yourself in the middle of an inappropriate action. In that moment you will hear your Observer Self clearly tell you that what you are about to do is not appropriate and you stop - thanks to this 'moment of awareness' - before you act from lack of balance. Taking responsibility for your actions requires constant attention and it works best if you do it seriously and consistently.

Let's say you are able to maintain this Self awareness. You are acting with confidence and you are experiencing Grace each day. Your payoff is more peacefulness and joy. Joy becomes your new internal template and you magnetize a life filled with rich blessings and amazing people. A gracious life is not characterized by raw pain and drama. Feelings such as jealousy, rage, terror, and greed have been already predominantly addressed and healed. Most people who do this work will still experience these emotions to some degree. The difference is that they are not controlled by them. As negativity leaves your personal template, you are less likely to attract physical manifestations of negativity in your future. This is truly up to you.

"Whatever you focus on gets bigger." This is such an important principle and it is so true. If you stay focused on the Grace in your life, you will experience even more Grace. If you wake up each morning with gratitude for being alive and for everything around you, you will have an even more astounding day. It is that simple. Do not question this principle. If you can not stay in "an attitude of gratitude," then question yourself. Ask yourself "why?" and work with those issues until obstructions dissolve and Grace comes forth again from the inside out. It is always available to you. You are the one who covers it from your own eyes. Use the state of Grace as a barometer. If you feel filled with Grace, you are in the flow with Source. Observe yourself daily, feeling to see if you are in the flow or not, and make regular course corrections to maintain your inner balance.

There comes a point in your evolution when you do feel filled with Grace and in the flow most of the time. This is the point where you are now "in the world, but not of it." This is a very powerful place to be. You are completely conscious of your Self and other people around you. You also know that your actions are not dependent upon others. You are an extension of Source with free will. You are aware of the collective unconscious and you are not easily swayed by everyone else's emotions. You are strong enough to stand in your Self (positive masculine) and vulnerable enough to stay open (positive feminine) to the world around you. With inner balance, you are able to make your own decisions, without drama, based on the total picture. This is mastery of inner balance and the goal of years of inner work.

Living in a state of Grace assures even more Grace. Again, "whatever you focus on gets bigger." Your inner template is the architect of your world and you are the one who must take on the challenge of change if you are not happy. Reiterating, this is a process that takes determination, awareness, and time. If you are humble enough to seek out your own flaws and willing to admit them to yourself and others, you have a chance to grow. If you are willing to let things 'Be' for a moment, then you make space for your feminine to come forth and express. Then, you can 'Do' what is needed.

The dance is about allowing and taking action, about Being and Doing, simultaneously. Loving yourself is staying focused on your template. Usually pain is the greatest motivator for change. But pain does not have to be the impetus. You can seek out positive changes and stay way ahead of the pain. You can step onto a wave of joy and ride it through any challenge in your life until you find that there are less and less challenges coming your way. Balance promotes more balance and more Grace.

Meditate on Grace. Meditate on what Grace would feel like in your body. Practice acting with graciousness towards others no matter what they do. Whenever your consciousness moves away from feeling the Grace in your life, let self-love stop you and correct your course quickly. See for how long, during each day, you can feel the presence of Grace. See how you can use the consciousness of Grace to deal with your daily challenges. Watch others around you to see how they respond to the new you.

Practical Exercises

The following Practical Exercises directly correspond by name and number to the Worksheets at the end of this book. It is best to look at the Worksheets when they are specifically described in this chapter. I would also encourage you to use large sheets of your own paper to write your own Worksheets, as you may need more space than is provided. You might possibly choose to use different colors of paper or pen inks to construct your Worksheets. If you can commit to completing all twenty Worksheets, you can feel confident that you have integrated a great understanding of the inner balance of masculine and feminine in your own life and in the lives of those closest to you. You will then find it easier and more natural to organically use these principles in your daily life. These exercises are the foundation of my practical workshops and DVD.

DEFINITIONS OF THE FOUR ARCHETYPES (Worksheet #1)

Use Worksheet #1. The first exercise is best done alone. Start with a plain piece of paper and a pen. Divide the paper into four equal-sized boxes and label them as follows: positive masculine, negative masculine, positive feminine, and negative feminine. Sit and meditate for several minutes before writing anything. Meditate on the following questions and place your responses in the appropriate boxes. What is positive masculine energy and what are the corresponding human attributes? What is positive feminine energy and how does it manifest? Then, do the negatives for each. The goal is to have a clear idea of each archetype in your mind after completing this exercise.

You are defining how you feel about the essential nature of masculine and feminine. This will bring up old stories and emotions for you to re-experience and hopefully to work with in the future, as you go through the other exercises. Focusing on what you feel is 'good' and 'bad' about feminine and masculine taps into a deep place inside. Your feelings and beliefs have been colored by your personal experience with the opposite sex. What wounds have you experienced as a result of negative masculine and negative feminine input in your life? Many questions, and no doubt many emotions, will arise.

As you ponder these questions, the first exercise is already working. Emotional responses will arise as you simply try to define what is positive and negative. This is an indication of how charged we really are on the issue of feminine and masculine. After you finish writing as many positive and negative things as you can about the masculine and feminine, set your paper down and reflect upon what you have written. Allow yourself to feel your biases and preferences about masculine and feminine aspects of your life. Allow memories and feelings to pass through your body as you focus on this highly charged topic. Feel your emotional reactions and allow those feelings to pass through you with sound and motion. As well as writing your definitions for each of the four archetypes on Worksheet #1, write some of your emotional reactions and insights about doing this process on the back of the sheet.

Know how to spot these four archetypes (positive and negative masculine, positive and negative feminine). The key is to be able to instantly look at yourself and others to honestly evaluate which of the four archetypes is working in each moment. This is a way to get to better know Self. Several archetypes often express at the same time. They can be at peace or in chaos with each other. You can monitor your own ever-changing balance at any given moment by keeping your Observer ever-present.

Sit with these newly clarified concepts for several weeks. Add important items to the four boxes as the information is revealed in your life. Be patient and stay open to receive the guidance and record your results on this Worksheet. At some future time, you can re-visit your writing and see how your conceptions of masculine and feminine are changing. If you are gathering many versions or stories in certain boxes, it may be helpful to simplify the large number of examples into a few key principles. For example when looking at the negative masculine, you may write down screaming, kicking, punching, tearing out hair, and spitting on others. This is a little too detailed. To make it simpler, you might say 'physical abuse of others.'

You can spot these archetypes within yourself and see them in relationship with others. This awareness becomes your radar. This is the warning and planning system that you can eventually use in an automatic way to nurture and protect yourself (the ultimate boundary and navigation system). Each time you re-visit your Worksheet, be aware of how you are reacting or acting in terms of each archetype. This is how personal growth occurs, one day at a time.

It is helpful to share the previous exercise with your lover or a close friend who is willing to go really deep with you. (If you do not find someone else to do this with you, continue doing the exercises in this book by yourself.)

Ask your lover or friend to do their own four archetype Worksheets for at least two weeks and then meet and compare notes. The other person should do exactly what you have done by placing different attributes in four different boxes to define what, for them, are masculine and feminine qualities. As you will have done, your lover or friend will need to develop a working concept of each of the four archetypes and be able to quickly spot the archetypes in other people.

When enough time has passed, have an active discussion with your lover or friend. Try to agree about what positive and negative qualities exist within the masculine and feminine. See what differences you can find in your experiences and resulting attitudes. Discover how hard it can be to definitively place certain qualities into one or the other of these boxes. This conversation will take you quite deeply into an even richer understanding of the archetypes and open you to recognize all of the archetypes in people around you and in yourself. It may also be helpful to discuss your understanding of the four archetypes with other people to get feedback which will help you to clarify your understanding.

After completing this initial exercise, your lover or friend may become interested in doing all of the other exercises in this book along with you. It would also be interesting to have a group of people do the processes in this book and then meet to share insights. Regardless, it is essential for each reader to do the exercises alone with or without the active involvement of others.

ANALYSIS OF SELF
(Worksheet #2)

This exercise is best done alone. It can be considered a difficult process in that it requires brutal honesty. **Use Worksheet #2.** What are your weaknesses (negative masculine or feminine) and strengths (positive masculine or feminine)? Take inventory of your present actions, emotions, and thoughts and decide where to best place each of them into one of the four categories on Worksheet #2. Don't rush this process. Take several weeks to keep adding self-realizations. Deeper insights about yourself will come to you over time, especially if you have set this intention by committing to this self examination. Name your personal characteristics and write each one in one of the four sections of Worksheet #2. Then take time to study this sheet and see how you operate in your world.

Which archetype is your favorite way to express yourself? Which archetype do you revert to when you are under pressure? How does your personal will connect to Source? Which archetype usually makes the choices in your life? Look more deeply and feel deeper within yourself. Who are you, really? Which of the four archetypes is dominant on your internal level? Often the dominant internal archetype is different from the dominant externalized archetype. More honesty brings more transformation and more joy. As in the previous exercise, write your feelings and responses about your observations on the back of Worksheet #2.

In doing this process, I would like to make an important distinction. Describe yourself by only writing down who you are now. The present may be a result of the past, but it is not the past itself. It is very important to stay in the present. See your inner uniqueness, as you write. It's not about the future or about what you are going to become. It is about knowing yourself as you are now. All of your guidance, intuition, and mind are here now and can be open to receive. Since you are an ever-evolving being, you are always changing. To be useful now, you need to approach this exercise from your present state of being.

On Worksheet #2, list specific characteristics of your personality and soul and place each of them in one of the four boxes. Take your time and be honest. After you have written all of this down on your personal evaluation page, decide which box best represents your primary form of expression. This means that you notice if you are primarily externally acting out the positive masculine, the negative masculine, the positive feminine or the negative feminine. It is challenging to categorize yourself in this way, but remember, you are only evaluating yourself as you experience yourself right now. Things can change and, with your newfound awareness and freedom of choice, you can consciously manifest a new primary archetype. Place an asterisk and the day's date in the box which best describes your main external archetype on that date. Now, look at the boxes again to determine which box best defines your main internal archetype on that date and mark that box with a different symbol along with that day's date. Repeat this entire dual process over the course of the coming months and see how your primary inner and outer dominance changes.

After writing, sit with your concept of self for several weeks. Start to observe yourself in action. See if you are expressing as the person you think you are on paper. Re-define yourself through repeatedly doing this process until the process itself changes you. Use fresh paper for Worksheet #2 every time you re-evaluate yourself. See how you change over time as self-awareness grows.

Consciousness automatically brings positive changes. Whatever you hold in your unconscious and sub-conscious controls your manifestation in the physical world. So, whatever you can become more conscious of, you can consciously change. Strive to bring that which is less conscious up into full awareness so that you can make more conscious choices.

You can take this exercise further by asking several other people how they see you. Be ready for a big blow to your ego. It is very common for other people to see you totally differently than you see yourself. The process can be very insightful if you are mature enough to listen and grow accordingly. Stay aware. It is important not to give your power away to other people's opinions and it's important to learn by listening to others. Make notes on another sheet about how you are perceived by each person you consult.

ANALYSIS OF YOUR PARTNER AND
(Worksheet #3)

ANALYSIS OF TWO OTHER PLAYERS
(Worksheets #4 and #5)

Choosing the right people to evaluate is very important. First use your lover, if you have one. The intimate partner is the closest mirror to self and usually the most profound external source of information about you. Choose at least two other people that you find 'challenging' in your life. Challenging usually means that they bring out intense emotions in you or that you find yourself avoiding them. These challenging people know just how to push your buttons. Meditate for several minutes about who of your acquaintances will best serve you in this process. You will be surprised how quickly their names will come to mind. **Use Worksheets #3, #4 and #5.**

We will call these three people the 'players' in your life. Put your partner's name on top of Worksheet #3. (If you do not have a partner, pick someone else you feel close to.) On Worksheets #4 and #5, place the names of the other two people you have chosen. As truthfully as possible, evaluate each of them in the same way as you evaluated yourself using the four archetypes. Fill in the boxes with the different characteristics that they routinely use to deal with you and with their own lives. It will probably take several weeks to do this completely. Make notes about each of them on Worksheets #3, #4 and #5. Keep adding new insights about each person as these come to you. Look for possible similarities or patterns on your Worksheets #3, #4 and #5.

It has been extensively pointed out in the text of this book that the idea is to take responsibility for the experiences that come to you. You have allowed yourself to participate in these relationships. You have continued to interact with these people, regardless of the amount of pain involved. You are not a victim! You are a co-creator, and you will see this by being fully aware of the experiences you are drawing to yourself in the present. Stay with this exercise and honestly look at each relationship in a non-blaming way. This is the best way to learn from the exercise. Use your Observer to see the patterns and webs of relationships around you. Once you can really see the patterns, you can consciously change them. Please remember, this takes humility, kindness and perseverance. You can also use fresh Worksheets to periodically repeat this process to observe your evolution.

COMPARING ARCHETYPES
(Worksheet #6)

Take the Worksheets you have now completed (#1 through #5) and bring them together. Take a look at all of them once again. Use Worksheet #6 to take note of the similarities and differences between all the people involved, yourself included. How do these archetypal patterns compare to each other? Which member of the group is most difficult and why? How do you react or act in response to different types of archetypes? Which person is most like you or most opposite to you based on what you wrote on your own personal sheet? Write your responses to these questions on the back of Worksheet #6.

The key players in your life are your teachers. Watch, learn, and change your actions according to what is being mirrored to you. See these Worksheets as tools to evaluate your major relationships. These selected people, your players, provide you the mirror you have created to show yourself to you. See these players as your supporters and be grateful for them, even when they are critical of your actions. This type of analysis can continue throughout each day of your life. It is the ever-changing mirror image that is the evolving you and that is evolving with you. Repeat this exercise on a fresh Worksheet over time. Watch carefully and you will grow through your greater awareness.

THE MIRRORING EXERCISE
(Worksheet #7)

This exercise is done alone. Look through your Worksheets on each person whom you have evaluated. Before reading what you have written, close your eyes and allow yourself to visualize the other person in your mind's eye. Let the image of their face form in your mind. See their expression, as you would see it now. **Use Worksheet #7.** This mirroring exercise could also be called "the three things I dislike the most about _____." On Worksheet #7, write the thing that bothers you most about yourself and about the three players you have chosen. Leave space after each of the statements. Stop reading this book after this sentence and do what I have just requested in this paragraph before reading to the end of the exercise. Do not go beyond this point. Just write your 'dislikes' on Worksheet #7. We will not reflect until later. Please do this now.

When you have finished, read what you have written about yourself. Now, ponder for a moment and see how what you wrote about the other people (or the extreme opposite of what you criticize about them) is actually also what you do not like about *yourself.* In the space after the negative statements about the other person, write how those issues are mirroring (directly or indirectly) your own negative characteristics. Stay focused and attentive. Write only about the specific negative parts of yourself, not about the other person. This teaches you how to bring everything back to yourself. This is an excellent way to make changes and to stop blaming others and to stop being a victim.

Whenever you find yourself having a strong emotional reaction to another person, do this exercise and find out what is inside of you that is up for transmutation. Again, as in our previous exercises, if you want to take this deeper, ask other people to do the same process with you. See how you are a mirror for them. This shared exercise can build real intimacy. Always assume that the other person is specifically sent to you from Source to share something that is most appropriate in that moment. Take that concept into your heart and feel that Source supports you through other people, even when it is sometimes painful. You can also repeat this process with new Worksheets over time.

BOUNDARY SURVEY FOR YOUR PARTNER AND PLAYERS
(Worksheets #8, #9 and #10)

Take out all of the sheets you have written on the major players in your life. On the front of these sheets is a description of each person's positive and negative masculine and positive and negative feminine characteristics. Meditate on the boundaries you have or do not have with each person. Let yourself feel the level of comfort or discomfort that you have when dealing with each person. Ask yourself what truths need to be said to each of them that have not already been addressed or resolved. **Use Worksheets #8, #9 and #10.** Write your insights on the back of Worksheets #8, #9 and #10.

Make a plan to communicate directly with each person in the near future. When you meet, clarify your feelings about existing boundaries and how you would propose to create new boundaries to better serve you both. Actually discuss new boundaries or, if that is not feasible, unilaterally invoke the new boundaries in your future interactions with them. If you choose the latter approach, be willing to explain the situation when they turn to you and ask what is going on.

Once you make changes in how you define your personal boundaries and stick to them, people will notice. Honesty and calm communication go a long way. If people ask why you are acting differently, tell them that you have realized that your well-being depends on having better boundaries and that your new behavior is part of the process. Real friends will support you through these changes. It is very important to note how each person reacts or acts in response to your newly-stated boundaries with them. After you have observed for awhile, write the various responses on the back of their Worksheets (#8, #9, #10).

When doing the inventories of the people in your life, you may come across some tough situations. There are many people in the world who really do not understand these principles and who may not change for a very long time. Sometimes it is necessary to end relationships with people who refuse to try to understand how you are intending to live or who refuse to support you in your goal of Self awareness. If this is the case, it is usually best to end these relationships using clear communication (positive masculine).

Work with your observations to consciously change the quality of your relationships by being more aware and by communicating more honestly. Balance your own masculine and feminine to bring more clarity to your external relationships. Use your masculine and feminine energies in new ways and find a better balance between them. This improves the quality of your life. Always watch your boundaries and keep them mutable as your relationships mature. This is an ongoing daily process that brings a simpler and more joyful life.

TRANSMUTING JUDGMENT INTO LOVE (Worksheet #11)

Judgment is a product of the negative masculine and the lack of self-esteem. We must first be able to change self-judgment into self-love before we can love other people. It is very easy to fall into the role of self-critic and be brutal with ourselves. This is quite destructive and must be avoided. The way to change this pattern is to look deeply within to see where the self-judgment begins and to start to deal with it at that place emotionally and mentally.

Use Worksheet #11. This exercise involves watching your mind. For two weeks write down any negative judgments that you hear in your head about yourself. "You are ugly." "You have got bad hair." "You have got bad teeth." "Nobody likes you." "You are always late."

"You're fat." "You're always fighting." "You're stupid." If you have this pattern, you will hear it in your inner dialog. On Worksheet #11, write down all these judgments and keep it with your collection of exercises. This is the script of your 'victimizer self.' You also have a 'victim self' that continually hears all these judgments.

The second part of this exercise is to go into a room where you will not be disturbed for at least thirty minutes. For about fifteen minutes, read your sheet of judgments out loud with passion (over and over, up and down the list) for about fifteen minutes until the drama has lessened considerably. This vocalizes the 'victimizer self' (shadow self). This voice is usually angry and critical. Let it have a real voice and do not be afraid of your shadow or you will give it more power over you. This is much like turning the light on in the closet to see how big the boogie man really is. You might just find a clown laughing on the floor. It is far better to find out, than to live in fear.

Now, in the last fifteen minutes, feel the 'victim self.' This self is characterized by feelings such as shame, fear, anger, and grief. Just sit there for fifteen minutes and feel the effect of self-judgment. Without enacting a direct process such as this, often these feelings are not felt because the criticism comes as a sub-auditory dribble, one item at a time. Now, you have just dumped so many things on yourself at one time and you really can feel it all. Over the next two weeks, repeat these 'victimizer' and 'victim' processes three times. Then you will then be prepared for the final step.

Do the last part of this exercise for at least four months to reverse negative beliefs. Write new positive affirmations specific to each negative statement you made about yourself. For example, if you said "I am always late," you can write something like this: "Because I'm always on time, my life works perfectly." Next time you hear yourself say something negative about yourself, stop and say the specific positive affirmation. Affirm that you make the choice to see yourself positively. Whatever you focus on gets bigger. If you continue the process for at least four months, it will work to alter your experience.

It is also important to heal any guilt about your past experiences. It is helpful to hold the following statement in your mind, "I have no regrets; no regrets for anything I have ever done." This may seem extreme, but you can not beat yourself up for what you have already done and for what can not be changed. The past is gone. You must forgive yourself. Life will work better when you have forgiven yourself for everything you have ever done that you did not like. The healing of guilt requires a lot of smaller processes. When regrets come into your consciousness, shift your negative belief system. Consciously affirm that you will make different choices in the future. Then, you have to follow through on your promises. These are promises that you make to yourself. When you do what you promise, you will feel better about yourself since you are meeting your new expectations.

Again, it is a choice in consciousness. Take full responsibility for your actions without guilt while continuing to act more consciously. Stop judging yourself and other people. Love people and know that some of them are innocent in their simple ignorance. Because they are unaware of their own problems, they are too unconscious to change. Compassion comes when you do not hold unrealistic expectations about others. "No expectations, no loss." It is compassionate to understand that some people do not know what is appropriate and will probably never change. Be patient and have compassion. This choice allows you to remain in a state of Grace.

With a little practice, you will be able to remain in states of great joy for days as you accept people for who they are. Not having to change things takes away a huge amount of pressure. Acceptance is a state of non-resistance. Going with the flow is easier and you actually become positively charged by the experience. Everything in your life is there to help you. There is nothing to resist. This truth may take years to integrate, but it really does work if you can embrace it.

GRACE
(Worksheet #12)

To do this exercise properly, you must be in your Observer Self. Take a few moments to meditate on the meaning of Grace and the outplaying of Grace in your life. Focus on feeling Grace in your body. What does it feel like physically to be in a state of Grace? What does it feel like in your muscles? What does Grace feel like in your emotional body? What is the range of feelings associated with Grace? How much time during each day do you feel Grace? What type of people or events increase Grace or decrease it? How long does it take to regain Grace after you fall away for awhile? Do other people seem to exhibit Grace in your presence? Keep watching with your Observer.

Practicing being aware of how Grace feels in your physical body allows you to move more consciously towards that state of being at will.

Use Worksheet #12. Write the word "Grace" on the top. Using the pointer questions above, make notes on your experience of Grace over a period of time. Write down what you are feeling in your body when you embrace Grace. Keep track of the type of events and people that encourage you to feel Grace. This is a way to acknowledge your appreciation for them. It is very good to develop your awareness to the point of being able to see how some seemingly 'negative experiences' on your list of things actually have helped to promote more Grace in the long term. As your inner balance becomes more refined, you will experience longer and longer periods of Grace each day. Eventually, you will find that every experience brings more Grace and clarity.

LAYERING OF EMOTIONS OF SELF, PARTNER, AND PLAYERS (Worksheets #13, #14, #15 and #16)

Use Worksheets #13, #14, #15 and #16. Consciously watch yourself in your interactions with the players in your life by using your Observer on a daily basis. Identify which of your emotions are regularly expressed to other people. Identify which emotions you hold within and do not share with others. Also determine this for the players in your life. Write these awarenesses on Worksheets #13, #14, #15, and #16.

Internal emotions that are not so easily shared or exposed to others, will be more difficult to identify. The easiest way to find these inner emotions is to stop yourself when you are acting out your usual external emotions. Stop and honestly ask yourself what is going on inside you emotionally at that moment. Be brutally honest with yourself. What are you really feeling, secretly, within? Keep practicing this process. It is often helpful to ask one of the players in your life to sit down and be honest with you about how they perceive you. If you can stay open to the process, it can speed your growth. To identify these layers for the players in your life, you will have to rely upon your intuition, aided by your Observer Self.

Repeat this exercise over an extended period of time. Write down your patterns of expressing different emotions in different situations. See how those emotions fall in predictable layers, the more 'acceptable' ones more easily expressed, while deeper, more painful feelings, tending to remain hidden. You will typically go through emotions in a certain order when under pressure.

For example, Jack is forty years old and manages fifteen workers at his auto assembly plant. Jack was severely physically abused by his father in his early teenage years. Jack has not been to therapy or worked on this issue of abuse with anyone throughout his adult life. At work these days, he is a very quiet man who states his orders to co-workers in a slightly abrupt and controlling manner. If he does not get what he wants, Jack starts to scream violently. When his superiors have had to intervene during these rages, Jack begins to act crazily and makes irrational comments. Yet, beneath all of those emotional layers is a terrified teenage boy. If Jack were to consciously work with his inner child terror, the other inappropriate emotional reactions would probably not occur in the future.

As you become more aware of your reactions to life, you will see which of your own layers are operating in each moment. Then you can consciously bypass superficial emotions and choose to do therapy or processing of the deeper layers. Observe how you use superficial emotional states to keep other people away rather than establishing healthy boundaries. Observe how others respond to your false layers versus how they respond to your real truth. The emotional patterns exhibited by the players in your life will also mirror these layers.

CHANGING REGRETS INTO ACTIONS (Worksheets #17, #18, #19 and #20)

Regret is always about the past. As long as the past is your focus, things will not change. Acceptance of Self is the way to change the belief in victimization into an understanding of being a co-creator with Source. In this exercise, you have the opportunity to specifically change your regrets into new choices for the present and future. A series of conscious choices becomes a lifetime filled with Grace and knowingness.

Use Worksheets #17, #18, #19 and #20. Look at your previous Worksheets to see what you have written about yourself and your three players. Try to feel the essence of each relationship by looking at this entire collage, seeing yourself and these players and what in you has brought them into your life. This will remind you of how unique each person is and how, using this system, you can evaluate yourself using anyone who appears in your life.

On Worksheets #17, #18, #19 and #20, write down what you have regretted not Being or Doing, for yourself and with each player. Remember, these are your regrets about either inaction or imbalanced action. What have you regretted not Being or Doing for yourself? For others? This process will take time. You may need to go back and add things to the list over the course of weeks as things come to you intuitively. Also begin to think about and feel how you could act differently in the future. See if you can use your intention to formulate a list of 'new' responses or actions.

Using these same Worksheets (#17, #18, #19 and #20) write your lists of your intended actions. What are practical things you can do to work with the specific regrets that you have listed for yourself and each person? These actions can be translated into real world activities (positive masculine) that you need to do to resolve the regrets. This is the beginning of taking real responsibility, and the path to becoming a co-creator. As you begin to make these changes, it is vital that your intuitive nature (positive feminine) stay active in this process. Masculine and feminine, Doing and Being, must act as partners. Your positive feminine can guide your actions, making sure you are staying on your intended course both with self and others. Everything you need to know is within you. Listen! Periodically check in with yourself and you will see that the number of your regrets is lessening.

Externalizing Inner Balance

Inner balance will only take us so far. It is perfect in theory and we may perfectly understand the theory. The next step is practice. In order to manifest that perfected union into the physical world, we must externalize the new balance that we have worked so long to develop. This is how we bring Source into manifestation on Earth. This is embodying Source in flesh and the only way to finish the process of externalizing inner balance. It is also the only way to be sure that we really are developing balance within.

The perfect arena to start exploring how you can externalize your new-found awareness is in your relationship with your lover, if you have one, and if not, with whomever you share your life most intimately. Start the process by remembering that even though you are each of a specific gender, you and your partner have both masculine and feminine aspects. Acknowledge that all parts are equally valuable and needed. You have already learned how to observe your own masculine and feminine in action and have learned how they interact with each other. You already have developed the skills to alter your inner template to more readily bring the balance you desire into your life. You have practiced and watched all of this play out with other people in times of joy and under pressure. You are well-prepared to expand your positive experience by externalizing your inner balance in your relationship with your lover.

The key is still Observation. As you act, you observe yourself and your partner's response. That response will influence your next action because you are conscious within the situation and fully in the present. This is a dance and you are learning the steps. You are discovering which of your actions bring reactions and which of your actions bring Grace as a result of how well-balanced you are yourself.

You can extend this practice to work with other people more consciously. You can see how your self-aware actions allow an easy ebb and flow between you and the other person on a moment to moment basis. This is real sensitivity and exemplifies the maturing of your consciousness. There is wisdom in taking personal responsibility for yourself and observing the effect mirrored back to you in your relationships with your lover, your friends, or anyone who appears in your life.

Be aware of how you are externalizing your inner balance. For instance, if you have defined yourself as shy, start by watching how shyness affects your behavior. Write down the specific behaviors you use to deal with other people and situations due to your self-concept. Once you are fully conscious of these behaviors, you will no doubt see that you are receiving similar responses from others, or the extreme opposite. This feedback can give you the incentive to choose new responses for yourself that are more effective. In this way you can use inner balance analysis to become more conscious of your actions and then you can consciously change those actions.

By seeing how your particular dysfunctions play out in your life, you learn to consciously intervene and change your outcomes, which is very empowering. This awareness itself allows for more opportunity for intuition to positively affect the situation. It also places more responsibility upon those who are more aware. The increased intuition counterbalances and helps you to deal with the increased responsibility. By staying fully present in each moment, you are naturally guided by your intuition towards healing and increased well-being through both experiences that bring pleasure and those that bring pain. If you are open to following these simple intuitive directions, Source will lovingly be leading you down your own personal 'path of least resistance.'

The success of this work depends upon trusting your own intuition. Once you have the experience of access to Source, it is very likely you will be conscious of Source within you from that day on. The next consideration is what to do with the information. Let your Observer listen and really hear what Source is telling you. See this as a great opportunity to have private commentary on your life that comes to you live and in the moment. Remaining open to present material is pertinent to your ability to take the cues and change your actions. Your intuition is always offering input which, if you follow it, will allow things to go more smoothly for you.

There are few people that can immediately drop their old ways and follow in the way Source advises. Most people have major trust issues around doing what Source instructs, forgetting that their own intuition is their co-creative connection. This book offers a process for healing the emotional, mental, and subtle pain which keeps us from trusting what we know. Pain must be healed in order to open to Source. Once your deepest issues have been addressed, then your Observer can become available to know what Source is suggesting, and you are free to explore new behaviors instead of re-enacting old patterns.

If you have doubts that the 'voice' you are hearing is truly from Source, one thing to remember is "the Voice never flatters." Take your time and feel deeply within yourself. Determine if the advice is ethical and based on love. Determine if the advice brings peace, simplicity, and less drama. These are a few simple ways to quickly judge if what you are experiencing supports your inner balance. Your Observer must remain ever-vigilant and you must be willing to hear, "No, that's not working for me." The positive masculine can be abrupt and extremely direct at times in order to protect self.

Let's say you have done the necessary healing and you are beginning to feel a connection to Source. Now, start to listen and gradually start to take the advice in areas of your life that are already fairly uncomplicated. Observe what happens. Do things get easier? Do you avoid problems by paying attention to your intuition? Do you reach out to others due to suggestions from Source? Source opens you up to a whole new world of possibilities and a whole new way of evaluating your actions and non-actions. Once you are confident that you are in tune with the real Voice of Source, begin to listen for it and use it in all areas of your life.

As a final example, let's examine how a person might react to the competing voices of self and intuition. Let's say, your tax return is due. Source, through your own intuition, says, "Get up off the sofa and go into your office and finish your tax return." That kind of statement could set off an internal war. You can only imagine what the shadow would say or maybe what the thirteen year old inner child would shout, while your inner masculine is saying, "That's right. We need to get it done. Get up now." During this entire 'exchange' of competing voices, your tendency is to lose touch with what is going on around you. You have gone completely internal. You have abandoned the present time. Parts of you are exchanging deep dialog. You are present with that dialog and not present in the room or even in the car you may be driving. This is when accidents are more likely to happen.

Even though the intuition is the unfailing guide and always offers advice or information in your best interests, you may still not follow through with what is being said. The message has to work its way through the chain of command from the intuition down to the will in order to perform the action. Your old patterns and dominant 'voices' will try to influence you. You must be vigilant to watch that 'you' are not the one who gets in the way. Perfection is guaranteed if you can step out of your own way and allow Source, through the voice of your own intuition, to lead the way. Eventually you learn to be humble enough to be wrong. Intuition knows a better way than your personal will does. Surrender control to Source through your ever-present Observer.

This is Grace in action. This is the goal. This is what you have been looking for. It is time to remove your veils and claim yourself as co-creator with Source. You have veils of ignorance (negative masculine), veils of emotional baggage (negative feminine), and veils of unfocused intentions (negative masculine). There is nothing intrinsically wrong with you. You have simply been unaware of your true nature and strength. Your intuition (positive feminine) will guide you into your own 'unveiling' if you can step out of the way. Remember, what is real is usually simple. Being aware of and acting from your intuition can reduce the complexity and drama of life. This is a science of consciousness that allows us to see ourselves through the 'mirror-like wisdom' of our reflection in other people.

Remain ever vigilant and look deeply into all aspects of your Being. Make new choices from this place of knowing the broader truth. Start living your life in 'broadband width.' See beyond your previous limitations by balancing your inner masculine and feminine aspects and externalizing that new balance into a more Grace-full life. The secrets of the Universe are inside you. Use what you know to change your life and you will positively affect your life and the lives of those around you.

WORKSHEETS

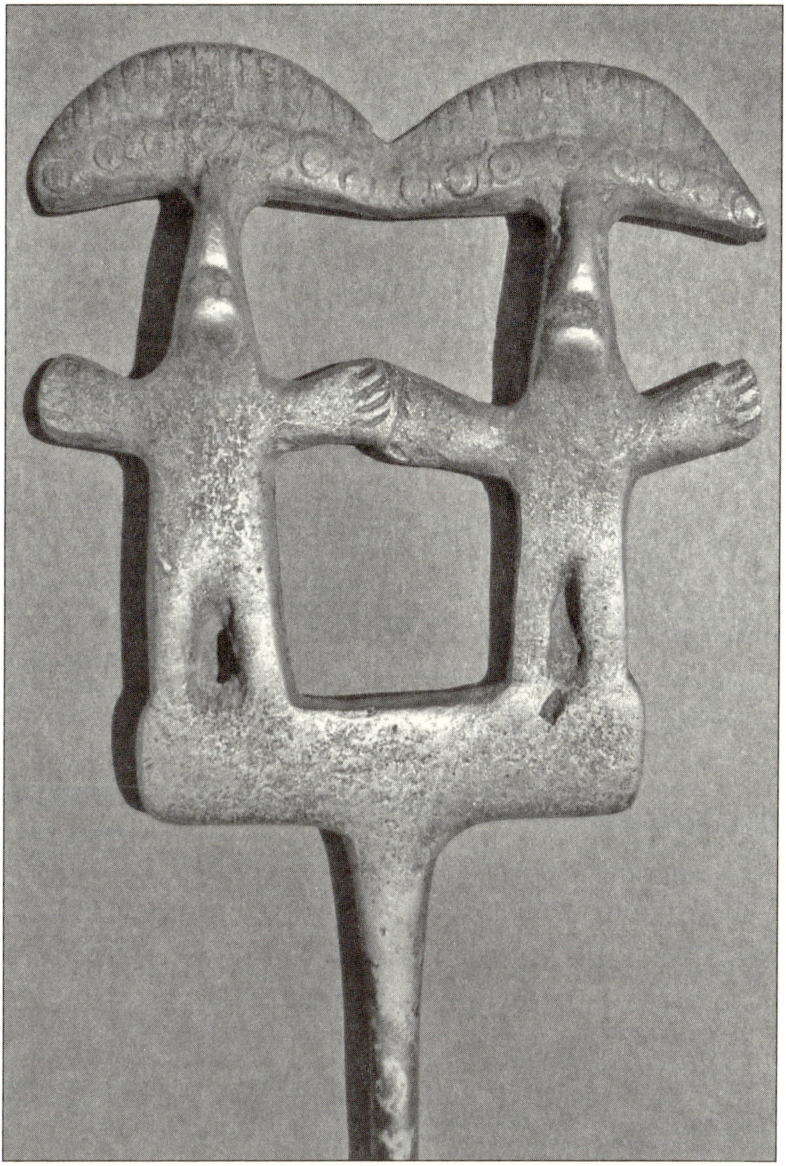

WORKSHEET #1: DEFINITIONS OF THE FOUR ARCHETYPES

LIST QUALITIES, EMOTIONS, AND ACTIVITIES IN EACH CATEGORY. USE THIS SHEET TO DEVELOP YOUR OWN SENSE OF WHAT EACH ARCHETYPE MEANS TO YOU.

POSITIVE FEMININE (STRENGTHS)

NEGATIVE FEMININE (WEAKNESSES)

POSITIVE MASCULINE (STRENGTHS)

NEGATIVE MASCULINE (WEAKNESSES)

Worksheet #2:
ANALYSIS OF SELF

List your emotions, activities, interests, actions, non-actions, and life situations in these four boxes based on how you defined the archetypes on Worksheet #1.

POSITIVE FEMININE (Strengths)

NEGATIVE FEMININE (Weaknesses)

POSITIVE MASCULINE (Strengths)

NEGATIVE MASCULINE (Weaknesses)

Mark the archetype which best describes your dominant external expression with * and date. Mark the archetype which best describes your dominant internal experience with # and date.

WORKSHEET #3:
ANALYSIS OF YOUR PARTNER

LIST YOUR PARTNER'S EMOTIONS, ACTIVITIES, INTERESTS, ACTIONS, NON-ACTIONS, AND LIFE SITUATIONS IN THESE FOUR BOXES BASED ON HOW YOU DEFINED THE ARCHETYPES ON WORKSHEET #1. (IF YOU DO NOT HAVE A PARTNER, USE THE PERSON YOU FEEL CLOSEST TO.)

POSITIVE FEMININE (STRENGTHS)

NEGATIVE FEMININE (WEAKNESSES)

POSITIVE MASCULINE (STRENGTHS)

NEGATIVE MASCULINE (WEAKNESSES)

MARK THE ARCHETYPE WHICH BEST DESCRIBES THIS PERSON'S DOMINANT EXTERNAL EXPRESSION WITH * AND DATE. MARK THE ARCHETYPE WHICH BEST DESCRIBES THIS PERSON'S DOMINANT INTERNAL EXPERIENCE WITH # AND DATE.

WORKSHEET #4:
ANALYSIS OF PLAYER 1

List this person's emotions, activities, interests, actions, non-actions, and life situations in these four boxes based on how you defined the archetypes on Worksheet #1.

POSITIVE FEMININE (Strengths)

NEGATIVE FEMININE (Weaknesses)

POSITIVE MASCULINE (Strengths)

NEGATIVE MASCULINE (Weaknesses)

Mark the archetype which best describes this person's dominant external expression with * and date. Mark the archetype which best describes this person's dominant internal experience with # and date.

WORKSHEET #5:
ANALYSIS OF PLAYER 2

List this person's emotions, activities, interests, actions, non-actions, and life situations in these four boxes based on how you defined the archetypes on Worksheet #1.

POSITIVE FEMININE (Strengths)

NEGATIVE FEMININE (Weaknesses)

POSITIVE MASCULINE (Strengths)

NEGATIVE MASCULINE (Weaknesses)

Mark the archetype which best describes this person's dominant external expression with * and date. Mark the archetype which best describes this person's dominant internal experience with # and date.

WORKSHEET #6:
COMPARING ARCHETYPES

Compare and contrast yourself with your three players by comparing dominant archetypes. Write notes on each person.

SELF

PARTNER (or another player if no partner)

PLAYER 1

PLAYER 2

WORKSHEET #7:
THE MIRRORING EXERCISE

List the one thing you most dislike about yourself and about each player. List what it specifically reflects back to you about yourself, either directly or oppositely. Write down what you have learned about yourself through mirroring.

SELF

REFLECTIONS ON SELF

PARTNER (or another player if no partner)

REFLECTIONS ON SELF

PLAYER 1

REFLECTIONS ON SELF

PLAYER 2

RELECTIONS ON SELF

Worksheet #8:
BOUNDARY SURVEY FOR PARTNER

Answer each question in regard to the boundaries you do and do not currently have with your partner (or another player if you do not have a partner).

1. How do you feel about the current boundaries you have with this person?

2. What more do you need to communicate to this person to have better boundaries?

3. Name the new boundaries that you would like to establish with this person.

4. How do you intend to communicate the new boundaries to this person? What is your action plan?

Worksheet #9:
BOUNDARY SURVEY FOR PLAYER 1

Answer each question in regard to the boundaries you do and do not currently have with this person.

1. How do you feel about the current boundaries you have with this person?

2. What more do you need to communicate to this person to have better boundaries?

3. Name the new boundaries that you would like to establish with this person.

4. How do you intend to communicate the new boundaries to this person? What is your action plan?

Worksheet #10:
BOUNDARY SURVEY FOR PLAYER 2

Answer each question in regard to the boundaries you do and do not currently have with this person.

1. How do you feel about the current boundaries you have with this person?

2. What more do you need to communicate to this person to have better boundaries?

3. Name the new boundaries that you would like to establish with this person.

4. How do you intend to communicate the new boundaries to this person? What is your action plan?

WORKSHEET #11:
TRANSMUTING JUDGMENT INTO LOVE

1. For two weeks listen for anything negative you hear about yourself in your own mind. List each of those things in this section.

2. List a strong specific positive affirmation for each negative thought listed in section one above.

Worksheet #12:
GRACE

Answer the following questions about yourself. Use the answers to invite the state of Grace into your personal experience.

1. How does the experience of Grace feel in your emotional body?

2. How does the experience of Grace feel in your physical body?

3. What events increase your experience of Grace?

4. Which people increase your experience of Grace?

5. What "negative experiences" have eventually resulted in the experience of Grace?

Worksheet #13:
LAYERING OF EMOTIONS OF SELF

ANSWER THE FOLLOWING QUESTIONS IN ORDER TO DETERMINE WHICH EMOTIONAL LAYERS EXIST. THIS IS INTENDED TO BRING MORE AWARENESS.

1. WHAT IS YOUR MOST COMMON OUTWARDLY EXPRESSED EMOTION?

2. WHAT INNER EMOTIONS DO YOU NOT USUALLY EXPRESS?

3. WHAT IS YOUR INTERNAL AND EXTERNAL WAY OF HANDLING STRESS?

4. LIST YOUR LAYERS OF EMOTION FROM THE MOST SUPERFICIAL TO THE MOST SECRETLY HELD WITHIN.

Worksheet #14:
LAYERING OF EMOTIONS OF PARTNER

Answer the following questions in order to determine which emotional layers exist. This is intended to bring more awareness.

1. What is this person's most common outwardly expressed emotion?

2. What inner emotions does this person not usually express?

3. What is this person's internal and external way of handling stress?

4. List this person's layers of emotion from most superficial to most secretly held within.

Worksheet #15:
LAYERING OF EMOTIONS OF PLAYER 1

Answer the following questions in order to determine which emotional layers exist. This is intended to bring more awareness.

1. What is this person's most common outwardly expressed emotion?

2. What inner emotions does this person not usually express?

3. What is this person's internal and external way of handling stress?

4. List the layers of emotion from most superficial to most secretly held within.

Worksheet #16:
LAYERING OF EMOTIONS OF PLAYER 2

ANSWER THE FOLLOWING QUESTIONS IN ORDER TO DETERMINE WHICH EMOTIONAL LAYERS EXIST. THIS IS INTENDED TO BRING MORE AWARENESS.

1. WHAT IS THIS PERSON'S MOST COMMON OUTWARDLY EXPRESSED EMOTION?

2. WHAT INNER EMOTIONS DOES THIS PERSON NOT USUALLY EXPRESS?

3. WHAT IS THIS PERSON'S INTERNAL AND EXTERNAL WAY OF HANDLING STRESS?

4. LIST THIS PERSON'S LAYERS OF EMOTION FROM MOST SUPERFICIAL TO MOST SECRETLY HELD WITHIN.

Worksheet #17:
CHANGING REGRETS INTO ACTIONS FOR YOURSELF

LIST SPECIFIC REGRETS YOU HAVE ABOUT YOUR OWN PAST ACTIONS OR INACTIONS. DETERMINE SPECIFIC ACTIONS TO RESOLVE EACH REGRET.

REGRETS ABOUT YOURSELF

ACTIONS TO RESOLVE REGRETS

Worksheet #18:
CHANGING REGRETS INTO ACTIONS FOR REGRETS WITH YOUR PARTNER

List specific regrets you have regarding your own past actions or inactions in relation to this person. Determine specific actions to resolve each regret.

REGRETS REGARDING YOUR PARTNER

ACTIONS TO RESOLVE REGRETS

Worksheet #19:
CHANGING REGRETS INTO ACTIONS
FOR REGRETS WITH PLAYER 1

List specific regrets you have regarding your own past actions or inactions in relation to this person. Determine specific actions to resolve each regret.

REGRETS REGARDING PLAYER 1

ACTIONS TO RESOLVE REGRETS

Worksheet #20:
CHANGING REGRETS INTO ACTIONS
FOR REGRETS WITH PLAYER 2

List specific regrets you have regarding your own past actions or inactions in relation to this person. Determine specific actions to resolve each regret.

REGRETS REGARDING PLAYER 2

ACTIONS TO RESOLVE REGRETS

Dissolution is the secret of the Great Work!

www.vitohemphill.com